The Odyssey of an African Slave

UNIVERSITY PRESS OF FLORIDA

Florida A&M University, Tallahassee
Florida Atlantic University, Boca Raton
Florida Gulf Coast University, Ft. Myers
Florida International University, Miami
Florida State University, Tallahassee
New College of Florida, Sarasota
University of Central Florida, Orlando
University of Florida, Gainesville
University of North Florida, Jacksonville
University of South Florida, Tampa
University of West Florida, Pensacola

Jack Smith in his minister clothes.
Harper's New Monthly Magazine, Harper &
Brothers, New York, New York, 1875.

The ODYSSEY OF AN AFRICAN SLAVE

By Sitiki

Edited by Patricia C. Griffin

University Press of Florida

Gainesville/Tallahassee/Tampa/Boca Raton
Pensacola/Orlando/Miami/Jacksonville/Ft. Myers/Sarasota

Copyright 2009 by Patricia C. Griffin, excluding the narrative.
Printed in the United States of America on acid-free, recycled paper

14 13 12 11 10 09   6 5 4 3 2 1

Library of Congress Cataloging-in-Publication Data
Sitiki, d. 1882.
The odyssey of an African slave / by Sitiki ; edited by Patricia C. Griffin.
p. cm.
Includes bibliographical references and index.
ISBN 978-0-8130-3391-4 (alk. paper)
1. Sitiki, d. 1882. 2. Slaves—United States—Biography. 3. Slavery—Florida—History—19th
century. 4. Slaves—Florida—Saint Augustine—Biography. 5. Freedmen—Florida—Saint
Augustine—Biography. 6. Methodist Church—Florida—Saint Augustine—Clergy—
Biography. 7. Saint Augustine (Fla.)—Biography. 8. Africa, West—Biography.
I. Griffin, Patricia C. II. Title.
E444.S53A3 2009
306.3'62092—dc22 [B]   2009019231

The University Press of Florida is the scholarly publishing agency for the State University
System of Florida, comprising Florida A&M University, Florida Atlantic University, Florida
Gulf Coast University, Florida International University, Florida State University, New College
of Florida, University of Central Florida, University of Florida, University of North Florida,
University of South Florida, and University of West Florida.

University Press of Florida
15 Northwest 15th Street
Gainesville, FL 32611-2079
www.upf.com

In memory of Jean Parker Waterbury
who discovered Jack's manuscript.

In memory of Sitiki
(later renamed Jack Smith in the United States)
who died September 3, 1882,
and of my husband,
John W. Griffin
who died in 1993 also on September 3.

Also, in appreciation of my Quaker ancestors
who worked for the abolition of slavery
in the seventeenth and eighteenth centuries
in Virginia and Maryland.

Contents

Preface

The African slave Sitiki, later named Jack Smith, is the centerpiece of this book. His narrative autobiography came to my attention in a circuitous manner. In the 1980s, historian Jean Parker Waterbury found a partial transcription of the autobiographical narrative among the papers of her grandfather, W. W. Dewhurst, author of *The History of St. Augustine* published in 1881. Determining that the narrative itself was in the Buckingham Smith Collection at the New-York Historical Society, she visited its archives and transcribed the handwritten narrative. Subsequently, she decided that I should undertake the publication. Her rationale was that an anthropologist would be better equipped to deal with the African context of the story.

I visited the New-York Historical Society on beginning the project in 1988. There, I found not just one full version of the slave autobiography, but two. In addition, I found a cleaned-up partial manuscript—about one-third of the total—apparently intended as a final draft that was never finished, plus some stray notes on various scraps of paper. The death of Buckingham Smith, the narrator's former master who was transcribing the narrative, probably prevented the completion of the third version.

Other projects and the writing of another book intervened before I could take up this work again in earnest fifteen years later. The impetus came through funding from the St. Augustine Foundation. The generous grant came by way of the Historic St. Augustine Research Institute, a consortium of scholars from the University of Florida in Gainesville and Flagler College in St. Augustine, Florida.

I am deeply indebted to a number of organizations and people for help in completing this work. Research was conducted at a number of institutions. The librarians and staff of the New-York Historical Society were gracious and helpful in working with the relevant materials. The help of the staff at the Research Library of the St. Augustine Historical Society was much appreciated, particularly the wise council of Charles Tingley, the library manager, whose knowledge of St. Augustine research materials is without parallel. Also, thanks to Joe Mills, volunteer of the St. Augustine Historical Society, who assisted with the graphic materials. The Georgia Historical Society, the South Carolina Historical Society, the Library of Flagler College, the New York Public Library, and the Greenwich Public Library in Connecticut were all useful resources.

Many individuals were helpful. My primary thanks are to Jean Parker Waterbury, in whose memory this book is dedicated and who passed away before it was completed. My thanks also go to the members of the Grant Review Committee of the Historic St. Augustine Research Institute that awarded the grant without which completion of this book would have been problematic: Kathleen Deagan and Michael V. Gannon—both of the University of Florida—and Thomas Graham of Flagler College.

Frequent conversations with Susan R. Parker enriched my understanding of St. Augustine history. Bruce Mouser provided many helpful suggestions on the African section of this work. Daniel L. Schafer, professor at the University of North Florida, also spent many hours helping me with the African section, even to the point of visiting and photographing the Rio Pongo area at his own expense and personal peril. The local men who took him up the waterway by motor required Schafer to row the three of them (head man, translator, and boatman) back against the tide when their boat ran out of gas. That long row to the settlement in the tropical, mosquito-infested mangrove coast certainly went beyond what would be expected of a colleague and friend.

Thanks also go to Sharon Lobello, who conducted research for the book at the South Carolina Historical Society. Canter Brown Jr., formerly with Florida A&M University, was generous with help on black history and the evolution of Methodism in Florida, particularly in St. Augustine. Also, not to be forgotten is the congregation of Trinity United Methodist Church in St. Augustine, the descendant of the church first founded by Jack Smith, Sitiki's American name, when he was still a slave. Thanks also to Bruce A. Gardow, my son-in-law and a United Methodist Church minister, for his insights into things Methodist, both past and present.

Continuing encouragement came from Jane Landers of Vanderbilt University and Bonnie McEwan at the Florida Department of State, who always believed that this slave narrative should be published. Elsbeth Gordon helped through consultation on architectural problems. David Nolan of St. Augustine constantly reminded me of the importance of the narrative to our knowledge of the black experience in Florida and of the need for wider distribution. Donna Ruhl at the University of Florida helped by putting me in touch with linguists specializing in West African languages. James Essegbey, also of the University of Florida, referred me to Valentin Vydrine of University of Saint Petersburg, Russia, who fixed on the slave's probable ethnic group and possible place of birth by using the African word list in the narrative. I am grateful for this valuable analysis.

I am especially grateful to Melanie M. Hunt of Cincinnati, Ohio, for sending me her ancestor's eyewitness account of St. Augustine during the Civil War, which includes material about the black experience in the town during that troublesome time.

To my late husband, John W. Griffin, and my son, Bruce Albert Griffin, I am indebted for technical research and other assistance. John aided in the initial stages by traveling with me to New York in 1988, sorting through the Buckingham Smith collection, putting the narrative on the computer, and even beginning the index. In 2004, Bruce aided me in New York by checking some items in the New York Public Library and scanning the images in one of the manuscript versions.

Lastly, I am pleased to acknowledge my debt to Sheila T. Harty for editing, proofreading, and computer troubleshooting, for putting the manuscript into proper form and, most importantly, for keeping me organized in this complex process.

Any mistakes, misinterpretations, or other problems are, of course, my own.

Introduction

A small boy, black in complexion, sat at the edge of a river with his bare feet kicking at the wavelets of water coursing through the reeds, tears tracking down his face. Seemingly, this scene was the Matanzas River in Florida, but it should have been a river in Africa. The rest of the scene was confused, as dreams usually are. When I awoke, I thought of the little statues of black boys fishing, common as ornaments on white establishments in the South during the early years of the twentieth century and of their ambiguous message.

When working on biographical material, the researched person becomes so real to the researcher that representations can burst forward without one's willing it. Whether such unscheduled phenomena help in the writing and analysis is a question. But if nothing else, they trumpet immersion and involvement.

Prior to the discovery of the following slave autobiography, no reliable accounts were thought to have emerged in Florida, particularly not one that covers sixty-five years of race relations in Florida's northeast region. This slave's narrative begins with his account of birth and life in Africa and travel to various locations in the United States before coming to northeast Florida when the province was still a Spanish colony. The slave Sitiki's long life—

from when the slave trade in Africa and slavery in America were legal to post
Civil War emancipation in the United States—adds a dimension without
parallel to our understanding of slavery as lived. Moreover, the information
furnished for the end of Spanish days in St. Augustine and for the Territorial period (1821–1845) enhances our understanding of life during two eras
that have received the least research attention in the long, rich history of St.
Augustine.

The narrative is remarkable in many other ways. Worthy of note is the
scarcity of confirmed narratives from American slaves, these accounts being
about fifty in number. Narratives of those who were born in Africa are a frac-
tion of that number. Some narratives claiming to be so are questionable.

Sitiki contributed much to his community as well as to his fellow slaves.
He initiated a black religious congregation and even managed to build a
church, both unusual for a slave in the nineteenth century. His accomplish-
ments are evidence of his administrative ability, hard work, and leadership.

In the genre of slave narratives, the document has both commonalities
with other such narratives as well as unique elements. The narrative is considered an autobiography—as others of this type are—even though it was
recited to and written down by another person, in this case, the former master Buckingham Smith. Although Sitiki could read, his ability to write was
limited. The account begins in the tradition of slave autobiographies with
the usual paragraph that sets the piece in motion, almost a formula for this
kind of literature. Sitiki, renamed Jack Smith under American slavery, declares himself a unique human being whose story others may like to hear.

The account that follows also has an element of adventure, particularly
in the part before entry into St. Augustine. As Marion Wilson Starling concluded, "Adventure is the chief stock in trade of the slave narrative from the
beginning to the end of its history" (Starling 1988:50). Certainly, as in Sitiki's case, being under four different slavery systems in six to eight locations
(depending on how one counts), captured twice during that time, and living
through several turbulent eras lends excitement and suspense to the narrative. Like most slave narratives, the document cannot be considered great
literature, but the spare, concise account carries its own elegance.

The narrative, however, has some differences from other slave accounts,
particularly in form. Essentially, the narrative is divided into three sections:

(1) experiences before 1817, (2) St. Augustine, Florida, at the end of the Second Spanish period, and (3) the last years of the subject's life. These three sections are unbalanced in length. The middle section encompasses 60 percent of the manuscript. Unlike other slave narratives that emphasize the life of the individual, this story has two different aims; to tell Sitiki's story and to provide a picture of St. Augustine in Spanish times and beyond. It includes in this description of the town the defenses of St. Augustine, its architecture, people, customs, and festivals. As St. Augustine is also the oldest continuously occupied European settlement in what is now the United States, a description of the town from the last days of the Spanish hegemony into the Territorial period (1821–1845) is especially noteworthy. Sitiki's description of life before coming to St. Augustine represents about 28% of the entire narrative, while the description of St. Augustine represents 62% and the wrap up 10%. Nevertheless, this last short section tails off in the middle of a sentence, thus, we will likely never know how many pages are missing.

The story of this remarkable black man was of interest to Buckingham Smith and his contemporaries. As a scholar of Spanish St. Augustine, Buckingham desired to put forth an eyewitness account of the town at the end of its colonial years. When the Smith family came to St. Augustine, Buckingham was only a child of seven years of age. Consequently, the adult black man who accompanied the child upon first entering the town could lend the account more veracity. Reading the narrative as dictated and transcribed years later, one visualizes two old men—one white, one black—sitting together and comparing memories of the town as it once was.

Buckingham's occasional rewording of Jack's rendition sets up static in the narrative, which is difficult to winnow out and is especially evident in the middle section. Nevertheless, one does hear the black man's voice, thoughts, feelings, and beliefs come through the words and veiled comments, particularly in the use of illustrative anecdotes.

Several elements of the narrative bear further comment. First, we must consider the trauma that Sitiki suffered after being ripped from his family and home at an early age and watching his father being killed. Before becoming an anthropologist, I was trained in children's mental health at the Institute for Juvenile Research in Chicago and then spent many years counseling children and adults and teaching graduate students in the field. From this perspective, I offer a few comments about the severity and effects of the trauma that the young Sitiki experienced.

The loss of parents and their nurturance is a severe psychic blow, yet the degree of severity varies among children. Any two children, depending on many factors, will react differently. One may have a severe reaction, which could even be classified as a post-traumatic stress disorder, whereas another child may experience a moderate reaction. From the sparse evidence that we have, Sitiki appears to have had a moderate reaction to the original trauma, which, while damaging, did not prevent him from leading a satisfactory adult life.

All other factors being equal, four elements contribute to a good outcome for children who have suffered a traumatic event. Those who overcome some of the worst effects are intelligent, cope well with unusual circumstances, remain in the same or a similar culture, and receive nurturing or comforting soon after the event. From what is known, Sitiki was clearly intelligent and coped ably with diverse circumstances throughout his life. Fortunately, he also stayed for a few years in a West African environment, associating with people who were of similar culture and understood his dialect. Essential to a child's recovery is nurturing available shortly after the trauma. Soon after his capture, the worn out and exhausted little boy was fortunate to be cared for and comforted in the village hut of his captor's wife, an African. The import of her temporary mothering to him is reflected in his telling comment after relating this story: "I got good treatment wherever it was my chance to go."

Later, Sitiki related to other substitute parents in a positive fashion. When he was a cabin boy on a slave ship, he tells us that he was treated "like a son" by Captain Brown. Later, when the captain needed to sell Sitiki, he made sure that the boy was not sold into a rice or cotton plantation but to a town merchant. Later, in adolescence, Sitiki related positively to the mother of his owner's wife in Connecticut and seems to have suffered in being separated from her when he was taken south again. Joshua Nichols Glen, the Methodist minister who converted Jack, was also a major influence.

Reaction to parent loss can take several paths. One is a constant search for parent figures with a consequent low self-image or, as in Jack's case, by becoming the parent figure oneself. He became the respected and loved "Father Jack" as the pastor of a black Methodist church.

Anger and acting out are elements that are displayed by children in Sitiki's predicament. We have some evidence that he was wild at play when staying in a hotel in Charleston. This behavior may have been a continuation of his circumstances on ship where he was not confined as the other slaves were. Also, we note the bird-stoning incident in Connecticut, where Jack took to heart the tearful reaction of his owner's mother when he presented her with a bird that he had stoned to death. In fact, the time as an adolescent on the farm in Connecticut was crucial for coming to terms with his enslaved status. He ends that section with the fatalistic statement, "These circumstances though not of interest to strangers stand out as everywhere important to me. The vicissitudes and movement of the family everyway concerned my own fortunes."

These adaptations to traumatic childhood events and subsequent enslavement combine with other elements to affect the narrative. One is the problem of memory at an advanced age, affecting both men with the shadings that inevitably occur through time. Another is the inclination to narrate a positive account to his former master by not revealing all his true feelings. These elements may have caused an intentional or unintentional masking, particularly of the negative aspects of the slave's life as chattel.

Additionally, the process of writing down this narrative is an odd blend of the oral culture from which Sitiki came and the literate tradition of Buckingham Smith. When Sitiki's voice is prominent, the stories focus on behavior and action, which reflect the cyclic repetition and variation of a life. Buckingham added a progressive dimension by blocking out time periods, bringing his former slave's stories back into a linear sequence, a technique which is evident even in the supposedly synchronic look at St. Augustine in Spanish times.

For the purposes of this book, two full versions of the manuscript were collated. Regrettably, the last fragment, which was the apparent beginning of a third and final draft, remained unfound as of my last visit to the New-York Historical Society. Some of the notes on stray pieces of paper were missing as well. Fortunately, I had taken notes in 1988 on the now-missing pieces. Buckingham Smith did not have the opportunity to polish "The Story of Uncle Jack," as he titled it, before ill health and death overtook him. A look at other drafts of Buckingham's historical work shows him as a sloppy writer with many strikeovers and rewrites before being satisfied with the final product (see Appendix B, "Condition of the Manuscript"). Thus, I have sifted through the various versions available to regain, as near as possible, the intended account.

What is presented here is an attempt to keep the narrative as close as possible to Sitiki's voice. The spelling and punctuation were not changed and neither were any of Jack's words deleted. In fact, in instances where Buckingham has evidently substituted more literary English for a colloquial phrase or African word, Jack's original word or phrase is brought forward again. For example, when Jack says that he went into the "bush" to pray, Buckingham has crossed out bush and substituted "woods."

Jack Smith declares in the first paragraph of his story that his speech is "broken and not entirely intelligible to strangers." Jack was probably conversant in, or at least understood, several African languages or dialects, English, Spanish, and the Minorcan dialect of Catalan spoken by a sizeable number of St. Augustine's Hispanic citizens. In writing down the narrative, Buckingham Smith must have taken the liberty to translate Jack's polyglot expression into clearer prose.

As the editor, I have needed to make a number of decisions as to the method of presenting the narrative. The first page, first paragraph, second sentence of the narrative illustrates differences among all the versions. One can read Buckingham's changes (in italics) to what Jack first said. The differences appear merely editorial and not substantive. So, although I have taken license in presenting one version, Chapter 1—the essence of "The Story of Uncle Jack"—is as accurately presented as possible. Among the sentences below, I chose the second. Decisions of this kind needed to be made throughout the narrative.

Version 1—I have thought myself therefore excusable in giving some written account of my life, inasmuch as my speech is broken and not altogether intelligible to strangers.

Version 2—I have thought myself therefore excusable in giving some written account of my life, inasmuch as my speech is broken and not altogether intelligible to strangers *who seem to desire hearing more of me than they learn.*

Version 3—I have thought myself therefore excusable in giving *in this way* some written account of my life, inasmuch as my speech is broken and not altogether intelligible to strangers who seem to desire hearing more of me than they learn.

Version 4—I have thought myself therefore excusable in giving in this way some written account of my life, inasmuch as my speech is broken and not altogether intelligible to strangers who seem to desire hearing more of me than they *know*.

Arrangement of the parts in this volume requires some explanation. After Jack's narrative, explanatory sections provide context for the reader. The early years of St. Augustine's history in the nineteenth century especially need such context in contrast with other periods of the town's history that have received more attention. Other sections interpret factual material and provide analysis of pertinent subjects, such as Jack's relationship with Buckingham, his religious life, and his attitude toward his enslaved status. For purposes of clarity, the slave's African name, "Sitiki," is used until he is renamed "Jack" at the time of his purchase in Savannah by Josiah Smith, Buckingham's father.

In examining the total manuscript, one sees a refreshing honesty in most aspects. The story is neither overly romantic nor a polemic for abolition, as many antebellum slave narratives were. Whatever the truth may have been about this man's inner life and attitude toward his enslavement, we will never know.

For those unfamiliar with honorific titles for blacks in the South, the use of "Uncle" or the female equivalent "Aunt" or "Auntie" was a mark of respect, a way for white people to distinguish some individuals as more deserving or to honor those who had reached a great age. Those occupying even higher status in the slavery system, especially preachers of the gospel, were referred to as "Father." Consequently, as the respected minister of the black Methodist Church in St. Augustine, Jack achieved that status.

From Sitiki to Jaques to Jack Smith to Uncle Jack and finally to Father Jack, I have followed this man through twenty years of my life. As an amusing coincidence while finishing this work, I am almost as old as Jack was when he died.

P.C.G.

I

THE PRODUCT
OF A LONG ASSOCIATION

I

The Narrative

[As recorded by Buckingham Smith and collated by Patricia C. Griffin from various versions at the New-York Historical Society]

The Story of Uncle Jack

Persons in San. Augustín who sometimes hear me address my brethren, children of Africans, and see me in the field with the hoe or gathering the fruit of my trees are interested from my advanced age to know somewhat more of me. I have thought myself therefore excusable in giving some written account of my life, inasmuch as my speech is broken and not altogether intelligible to strangers who seem to desire hearing more of me than they learn.

Of Kindred and Countrymen

I was born in an interior country of western Africa. At the age of four or five years I became captive to a neighboring people. At the time I had a father & mother and a brother a year younger than myself whom I used to lead about by the hand. My name was Sitiki, my father's Deva, my mother's Jene. The name of the little fellow I cannot recollect. The town that we lived in was

First page of the manuscript *The Story of Uncle Jack*. Buckingham Smith Collection,
New-York Historical Society. By permission of the New-York Historical Society,
New York.

large and had gates, the walls were of clay, as also were the dwellings. I have
seen no house of worship.

My father was a weaver; and I remember standing by him while he wove
cotton raised in the fields thereabout. I have seen him at prayer, kneeling on a
sheepskin, bowing to the earth, his head touching the ground, uttering words
not understood by me: "*Ala-ala-mama-lay sutta . . .*" or something like that.*

* with these western Africans the Arabic is the learned language which they study as we do Greek and Latin.

Probably the words are; there is

la	no
ullah	deity
illa	but
allah	the Deity
wa	and
Mohammed	Mohammed
Usool	the envoy
Allah	of God.

A.J.C.[1]

Elephants there were and horses. Cows, goats and particularly hair-sheep were in plenty. The deer were bigger than those of this country, their horns without branches.

The troops carried spears and swords, used bows and arrows, and some few had guns. Many of them were mounted. They blew on horns of ivory, beat drums, sang and played on harps, banjos & guitars. I remember seeing an instrument that looked like a piano. They were people very fond of music. They were all black, wore slippers and otherwise draped themselves not un-like our Indians.

Produce and Manufactures

Stone implements were not in use. There were no carts, and cattle were not harnessed to draw. Salt was brought to the town on asses in great pieces. Cultivation was with the hoe alone, which, like the axe, was of iron.

The vegetables of that country are chiefly yams, Guinea corn, rice, such corn as we have here, onions, large tomatoes and sweet, a root like a turnip, pumpkins, okra; of the fruit were bananas, plantanos, coconuts, oranges, lemons. I saw no pomgranates [*sic*] nor cabbages, neither sugar cane nor sugar. Honey is in plenty. Palm trees, white figgs [*sic*], tamarind bushes and fruits I have not seen elsewhere, grew in the wilds.

There were blacksmith shops in that town, saddlemakers and schools. The children learning by what they wrote on boards in a language I did not know.

Pots were made of clay & shells used for money. Gunpowder and soap were manufactured & leather tanned. There was little silver. Gold was employed in ornaments, particularly for women, who in general wore it as bands about the wrists, arms & ankles.

The Language & Country

I have tried since coming to America to ascertain the name of our people or of our town; but I could never learn anything. One African I talked with seemed to think that I was of a country called Mora.[2] The language I spoke is called Guinea. I remember some words.

Fire	*Bande* in Mandingo *taa*
Water	*gui*
Hand	*bulu*
Woman	*musu*
Knife	*muru*
Corn, maise	*seno*
Meat	subo
Horse	sho
Ass	shofala
Cow	sigui or ninki
Fowl	sese
Dog	wulu
Rice	coro in Mandingo malo

Of My Capture

It happened on a time that our little family, accompanied by a woman, went on foot about a day's journey to a village where we stopped. While there we heard cries of war with the report of fire-arms at a distance. The inhabitants ran into the swamp nearby. Directly a man entered our house and took the gold rings from my mother's fingers & the beads from her neck. Then another man came and took her away with the woman. My father arriving and seeing us boys hiding in the corner, took his sword and stood by the door. Two men came and told him to give up; he refused: they afterwards brought two men to talk to him. He then surrendered. One man took my brother, the other took me. After going a little way I looked back and saw a multitude of people around my father making a great commotion. I ever had the opinion that he was killed there.

Next day I met my mother on foot in a cavalcade at a crossroad. She gave me a handful of *pica*, ground nuts.[3] I was mounted behind the man who first took me. After she was gone, my brother was brought along on horseback following her, and I gave him part of my nuts, the man I was with riding *ufa* that I might do so.[4] I never saw either of them again.

Of My Captivity & Sojourn in Africa

We went to a town Seko or Sulko where the governor lived. The captives were set in a line, and his constable chose a few from them; the rest were taken away to sell. On the way we stopped at the place of the man who took me. The house was of one room, the walls made of sticks plastered with clay, the roof was of grass. (We were several days out.) I was unable to hold out longer. My head was bare, as it had been at home; my only covering was a little cotton sac. The wife was sorry for me, washed me with warm water and put me to bed. It was a mat spread on a sort of bench. Fortunately, people seemed to like me. I got good treatment wherever it was my chance to go.

I was carried in a canoe on a river, up stream I think, two men going with us. [Side note on second draft manuscript: "Men marked according to their nation."][5] We were out one night & day, arriving at a town where we tarried for two or three days. The governor there bought me and made a present of me to a man who took me down to where he lived. The inhabitants continued to understand me, their language differing only a little from that I spoke. Thence my owner took me to another town, a day's journey, where I remained with another man about a year. My employment was tending sheep.

Travel to the Sea

I was now to be taken with a male slave to be sold on the coast. Our company consisted of a half dozen men with guns. A priest of some sort traveled with us. He wore a dark gown and made use of a rosary. He did not offer prayer in our tongue. Before day and after sunset he ate and drank apart out of sight. On foot & sleeping in the woods we came in about a weeks time by an open road to the sea.

The country I was born in as well as that I had been over was everywhere stony. Some portions were mountainous and in parts water came in rivulets & fell in cascades. We had not once crossed a river. A day and a night before my arrival we came to the camp of a Fulah.[6] He owned herds and gave us cows milk with boiled rice to eat.

I remember as incidents of this journey that I saw a brown ostrich the size of a colt. He was confined in a house. When I first saw him I ran, never having seen to me so strange a creature. I once heard a lion roar at a long distance, yet to this day it has so chanced that I never saw one.

While on our way we espied three buffalos feeding in an open savannah. One was shot & we ate the flesh at night. While I sojourned somewhere in a town called Bambarra.[7] I heard that a wild elephant had been killed and I went to look at it. As he lay he appeared big as my house here. I tasted the meat, it was coarse and unsavory. The deer were larger than those of this country and the horns without branches. Goats and particularly hair sheep were in plenty. I have seen several camels. We passed somewhere through a town called Kissi.[8]

Arrival at a Barracon

Just before coming to the sea I beheld a white person for the first time. I scrutinized him closely to see what kind of being I could make out. His stay was short. He did not care to buy me as I was to be sold only with the man & he was old. Going on farther we came to an establishment by a river, eight or nine miles from the sea, where, when the tide went out, the beach was bare for a mile. There was a dwelling having a ball room I remember, gardens, beasts & poultry with everything for convenience and comfort. Here I first saw a store of goods. He took me then into his house for a servant, where I remained until his death. He breathed his last while I held his head. His name was Taylor.[9] His wife was a black. She afterwards went to England. A dozen or more white men attended the funeral. Their number surprised me,

I presume they were English. In a short time I was taken off to another like establishment. There I heard of Kingsley and Frazier,[10] names I became more familiar with afterwards in Florida where I knew one of those persons who owned Negroes here and plantations. The native people who live about the settlement are called Juluf.[11]

My Departure on a Slaver and Arrival in the Southern States

One day I was taken on board a brig anchored in the bay and sold to the master. Captain Brown took me into his berth and treated me like a son.[12] I was allowed to run about at large and do as I might please. In this vessel we came to America with a cargo of slaves. On the passage two men died. We had a doctor on board. The blacks received a pint of water each day and all the cowpeas and rice they could eat. Arrived in Charleston the Captain went to a hotel kept by a one armed man. I slept in the same bed as my master. We had to go from there before long, as I made too much noise at play. And the Captain was obliged to be about. We removed to the boarding house of Mrs. Ellis.

We next made a trip to Savannah, taking with us two slaves for sale. Here finding that he should have to go to sea again Captain Brown reluctantly concluded to part with me and in so doing it was his care that I should not get into a cotton plantation nor into a rice field. A merchant of the town came on board to look at me.[13] He was a large man, in blue coat and buttons, florid, some thirty-five years old, in the vigor of life. He liked and bought me. He asked me my name. I told him. He said it was no longer so, but Jaques. From that time I have borne no other name than that & his.

This occurrence was in the month of March of the year 1808. In no instance have I ever known the valuable given in exchange or the price for which I was sold. About a month later my master bought a Negro girl thirteen years old. My employment was to stay about the store, hers to tend upon the children. She is still in our yard.* [There follows a separate note written on the back of the page by Buckingham Smith]:

* The negress Judie, now far advanced in years, states that she comes from a town called Mayon, that war existed between her people & a neighbor-

ing one using a different language. While out with a brother, younger than herself, in the woods gathering wild fruit, they were surprised, their mouths crowded with cloth and bandaged, and being thrown upon the shoulders of stout men they were carried away by the enemy. They remained some years in the country after their capture and were then taken to the coast & shipped. Her name was Poli, her brother's Bayo. They separated in Charleston; she was sold in Savannah. She recalls in her native tongue the words (Spanish letters): *gulu* [hog], *brende* [dog], *ros* [rice], *chusu* [fowl], *yacha* [man]. It was never her fortune after parting with her brother, to find a person speaking the language of her country people. B.S.

A Voyage and Residence in Connecticut

My owner's family consisted of his wife, a son, Josiah, about two years of age, and a daughter an infant. In the month of June we all went North by sea, and arriving in New York took a packet to New Haven, whence we proceeded by stage to Watertown where my master and mistress were born. My occupation was the old one, to look after sheep & also tend the horse, look after and feed chickens, see to cows. For two months we staid at the residence of my mistress' mother, and afterwards at a house my owner built before going South. I am told the buildings still stand the more modern one altered the other preserved unchanged for antiquity. I can recall little of interest now that occurred there.

A single incident will detain me that has influenced to the full extent my after life. Having struck down a bluebird with a stone that I threw I brought it into the house and laid it before my mistress' mother. She moaned over it, spoke a few words and dropped some tears. From that time I could never cage or catch a little bird for any inducement, though many flit and build their nests about me of bright colors and sweet song.

We stayed in Watertown two winters & left in November to return to Georgia. Judie only remained, to take care of the little son of a lady, the infant child of our family having died. These circumstances though of no interest to strangers stand out in my lifetime as matters everywhere important to me. The vicissitudes and movement of the family everyway concerned my own fortunes.

Return to Reside in Georgia

We came to the town of St. Marys, Georgia in the year 1809 and in the month of October of the following year, 1810, we resided at the heights of Cumberland by the beach on the north side of the Island when vessels in sight go to and from the sound. We had gone there to escape the heats of summer, and where a son was born, the survivor of the family now many years.[14]

During the Embargo of Jefferson misfortunes attended us.[15] My master went with the family from St. Marys to Fernandina opposite, on Amelia Island belonging to Spain, leaving me in charge of his house in St. Marys a little way out of town. The British, then at war with us, having come there, the officers carried away the furniture and took me to their quarters. My master applied for me of the admiral, who gave consent that I should go if I chose, and Cockburn gave me a written license to pass where I might like.[16] Several hundred black people were induced at this time to take shipping in the English vessels with the assurance of freedom and embarked for Halifax.

On the day we received news of peace a young mistress was born,[17] in a house near the residence of "Old Fernandez," still standing on the bay, before what were his corn and cotton fields, behind the wharf at Fernandina new town. In time she became the wife of a surgeon of the Army.

Trivial circumstances seemingly unimportant come to be the tallies that passing over memory often connect for me in their order more to important incidents of life.

We Remove to Florida: City of St. Augustine

We returned after the war to live in St. Marys until the summer of 1817 when we removed to Florida. The vessel my master chartered having failed to gain entrance into San Augustine because of the westerly winds that prevailed for fully a week while before the harbor, they returned to Fernandina, and he, with the family, came on by boat and the land passage.

I returned again to the port in the same schooner, having the household furniture in charge, and arrived before San Augustine the 17th day of May. The city is behind an island 14 miles in length on the north end of which at the entrance to the bay is a white sand reef, covered with numberless sea birds.[18] A beach extends for a long way on either shore, and an advanced watchtower on the left approaching presented to me an appearance both new and interesting. The white flat-roofed dwellings of the town were seated in groves, behind the bay of azure, over whence at this season a fragrance of orange blossoms perceptible from our first drawing near the coast. The land side of the town was partly sheltered by breakwaters against the waves, which in tempests reached there from the sea. The pilot conducted us by the channel under the walls of the fort by the tower on the northeast corner,[19] where it was the custom to hail the arriving bark, and anchored the vessel out in the harbor.

The sun went down leaving vivid colors spread over the western horizon beyond distant pine tops. A simple drum rolls, and the flag on the castle, a red lion in a yellow field, floated for a moment in the air, and then came down from the staff.

On all other sides of the town, looking from the eastward, the land presents a fortified aspect. On the northeast stood the castle, mounted with the largest ordinance; thence westerly ran a mote [sic] the whole distance to San Sebastion Creek terminating with a redoubt called El Cubo. There two cannons were planted, and midway returning on the mote [sic] called the City Lines, was another cannon, mounted on a lesser redoubt. The whole embankment was staked with square posts eight feet high, the broad trench circulating water between the creek and the Bay taking the water of the fort through the eastern outlet. This line at the north end of the principal street contained the City-gate, which being locked at night the key was taken to the governor, and not again open until sunrise.

Along the San Sebastion going southward was a redoubt, with a cannon, at the end of an avenue running through town from the west, now commonly called Bridge Street, and further on was another redoubt where the shore projects and at present stands a saw mill, being a little beyond another highway passing from that creek to the eastward. This ordinance was placed to defend the openings through the marsh from any armed approach that might be attempted from the water on the west. Two cannon were mounted on the redoubt on the point at the south end of the ancient town, where the Maria Sanchez enters to divide the old from the new town, forming the little channel near the shore familiarly called El Poso, the well.

Exterior Military Fortresses

On the seacoast of the island opposite the City was a square tower commanding a view of the ocean. A stone house stood near to the eastward, and on the southern side, uniting the two edifices was a wall, enclosing a small yard looped for arms. Two spars erect on the tower, one on the north, the other on the south side indicated to the inhabitants of the town the direction and character of approaching vessels. The second staging of the edifice I am told was added by the English. An inscription let into the eastern wall, at the time it was made into a lighthouse by the American Government, entirely misleads.

The sea has here encroached within a hundred yards of the edifice, carrying away the land, the distance of a mile since the Spaniards left it.

The little castle on the islet in the bay of Matanzas was sustained from San Augustine,[20] and its garrison relieved once a month. Access to it, I have been told, for I never saw it, was over the wall by a ladder that might be let down or drawn up at pleasure. The same contrivance was in use at the post on the San Juan River,[21] directly west of the city of Picalata, having a stockade all long since gone to ruin. At the head of a creek called Moosa,[22] about two miles north of the town, was a small fort of which the walls, four or five feet above ground, may yet be standing. Other military stations existed, as on the plains of San Diego and the shores of the St. Johns, but I have no information concerning them.

Edifices, Municipal & Political, of the Revenue & Government

The building on the western side of the plaza was called the Governor's house. The last governor but one, White of whom we hear so much, lived and died in it. It was surmounted by a wooden cupola. The western side was of one story, with a flat roof. The entrance was by the court, through the portal, which on the exterior had two columns on a side. These are the yard and gateway of today. The ascent to the second story was into the piazza by the staircase leading up to it, at the entrance against the wall directly to the right. Two sections of those pillars are now stone seats under two of our fig trees near the dwelling . . . [illegible] . . . . The half moon that forms a portion of the stone fence on the back part of the lot on which it stands, I have understood, was a curtain or military work for the entrance to the City-gate at the time when the western limit of the town was here, close to the shore of the creek nearby. The stone house with arched windows at the northern corner of the first street running east and west in coming from the Castle along the water side was the King's Smithy. Along the eastern side of the town were two seawalls; the first extending from the Castle passed [*sic*] the second alley north of the Plaza. Except here for a few yards, the wall had been broken up by the storms, and the blocks of coquina were lying about cast on each other.

On the portion standing six feet high was a shaft of the same stone with an inscription already too worn by wind and rain to be read. Some dozen feet to the west of this wall, admitting the free passage of boats, between them to the beach, was another wall, which it overlapped. This other wall, standing unimpaired, reached to the plaza and turning inward, terminated at a short distance. The foundation of the ancient structure may be discovered within the present sea wall built when Florida had become a territory of the United States.

In speaking of the Castle of San Marcos, I acknowledge my inability to say much more than what addresses itself to its age. The [illegible] has been repaired and the wall stopped since the cession of the country to the United States. At that time (1817) the corners of the southeastern bastian [*sic*] had fallen into the sea. The glacis on the northern side had been dug away by the military, and some of interior portion had crumbled. On entering the *porticullis* [*sic*] the cell to the right was occupied by the guard, the cell behind it was the prison, and that still beyond, probably for ammunition. The first and second cells to the right were occupied by officers. In the middle of the first room and fronting the door was the King's Chest with three locks, the keys severally in the possession of the Governor, the Judge, and the Collector of the Port. Before the Civil War the lid of the box began to be chipped, and a large square piece sawed out of it, and little by little the whole has disappeared. In front of the entrance was a Chapel in which there is a fount against the wall. The priest was Michael Crosby,[23] an Irishman, whom I have had frequent occasion to hear converse. Two friars of the order of St. Francis attended the soldiery and after a year or two went to Cuba.

An edifice of the revenue,[24] apparently of an early date, was on the second corner of the block to the right on entering the street in the northwestern part of the Plaza. It was built on two sides of the corner, was of flat roof with embrasures and spouts in form of small cannon to conduct off the rain. The windows were large and broad with projecting sills and sides and were latticed. The walls are still standing with the stone arches, over which a wooden second story has been raised; but somewhat has been taken from the breadth of the corridor to enlarge the rooms. I have understood that a floor indicated on the eastern side a third side to the structure. The wall near the opposite corner of the street north having several pilasters appeared to have been intended for a house that had not been finished. In the manner this is built with windows I have heard that garden walls are sometimes made in Spain, the apertures having iron bars.

The City-gate is considered one of the latest works of the Spaniards. The gates were of wood in two wings, the heels resting on stone and held erect like a rudder of a ship by staffs in rings of iron. Soon after the cession of Florida an attempt was made by one of the early commanders at the Port to demolish the City-gate and he actually commenced work when his purpose was arrested by the corporate authority who claimed the fabric. The pomegranate on the summit of the western side was again set up with some portion below, and it will be noticed that there is no flower crown on it, as has the opposite, but is a cone.

In the midst of the Plaza is a monument the very last work of the Spaniards in Florida. It was raised to their constitution and was dedicated in my time, tho I did not witness the ceremony. The little blocks of marble were inserted, each inscribed Plaza de la Constitution. The largest tablet found recently in the town has since been introduced. It was no doubt intended for a dedication earlier than that which took place. A sign of square and compass below the lettering is worthy of remark.[25]

Structures Civil and Military

Near the street block in the north east corner of the public square stood a guard house where the city time was kept by sentinel and sand glass, and the hour struck on the bell at the market house. Within were stocks to detain delinquents until morning with air in full sight. At seven o'clock after dark the tolling of the great bell at the church announced the *Oracion* when people at once arose to prayer. The messenger in the street, carrying the written order between the ramrod and muzzle of his gun halted, or fell on his knees. After a few moments of silence, of cessation from work or pleasures, the people all again resumed their business or pastimes. From nine o'clock when the bells were chimed, until daylight, whoever passed that guard or approached a sentry within call was hailed, the cheery questioning being ever the same, and nearly the response.

"*Quien vive*?" "*España.*" "*Que gente*?" "*Paisano.*" Question: "Who Lives?" Answer: "Spain." Question: "What people?" Answer: "Countryman." The parley often caught subjects overnight that afforded entertainment for the early hours of the morning. On one occasion a guest of the Governor having staid over late, he was unable when in the street to give any account of himself, and enjoyed the King's hospitality until daylight, and that within a few doors of whence he had emerged only a few moments before.

[Below is a section on a separate piece of white paper in Buckingham Smith's handwriting describing Governor Jose Coppinger; a section evidently intended for inclusion at this point in the narrative.]

The courteous the refined Irishman who groomed us was a rigid disciplinarian & knew no friendship before his duty. I have seen him often, heard him converse & can say I know him. He was about forty years of age, of person full, graceful and rather short. Though sparing of amusement he was fond of society particularly of strangers. His manners were happy, his voice sweet and sounding in command. He was widely reported brave. After he left us, he held command of the castle before Veracruz where I have heard he distinguished himself holding for Spain the last ground left her in the country. [end of section]

[Also planned for inclusion here was the following, written on blue paper.]

His house, the best in town, has been burned, his modest residence has disappeared, but his voice calling "Enrique" and the answer of his orderly on the stairway below "Señor" are still in my ear. [end of section]

Of Religious Edifice and Burial Ground

The only house of religious worship at that time was the present Catholic Church on the north side of the Plaza.[26] When persons passed its portal they invariably lifted the hat until they had gone by. At this door the criminal sought sanctuary when closely pursued, and a guard was directly set over him until such times as the priest arrived, and delivered him over for trial to the proper authorities. I have understood that the building was put up about 80 years ago, which of course was after the Spaniards came here a second time, tho set upon foundations previously laid. On the opposite side of the green where the Episcopal Church now is, was standing when I first saw the spot the remains of an edifice in distinct outline above the ground. They said it had been an English church.[27] The Catholic burial ground on the quarter of town now called Tolomato existed as at present; and some monument there showed that it had been in use during the English possession. One of the monuments in form of a "*majonera*" is said to mark the grave of Gov. White.[28] The little chapel within is a modern structure. In the time of my coming into the country, there were some stones and hillocks that marked graves in an open lot a little south of Bridge St. on the east shore of Maria Sanchez Creek. It was represented as having been the burial ground of the English. A still older cemetery appears to have existed on the first lot or block of ground south of the market where a few years ago in preparing for the foundations of a house, were dug human bones, gold lace and wrought nails.

The convent of San Francisco then and now used as a barracks for troops has had no change made in its walls.[29] It has been three times since put in repair by our governor. The wooden quarters resting upon the wall on the western side of the court are modern. The part on the southern side, of stone, was probably the dispensary, kitchen and storehouse of original design. They were without roof when I first saw them and from the charcoal scattered about they appeared to have been burned.

Beyond the lines about six hundred yards north of the Castle on the furtherest side of the first creek making into the lands is a piece of rich, shelly soil, a little above the surrounding country. On it was said to have been a small church in early times for the devotion of the Indians, then the occupants of the country. That they lived on the lands about there as well as that covered by the town and every fertile spot is abundantly proven by fragments of pottery to be gathered. The stones of the foundation (of this church) still mark the outline of the little square structure. Sprouts from the stumps of an old fig tree grow hard by and I remember when the walls were of a good height they were occupied (with a covering) as a cottage having a garden about them and some fruit trees.[30]

Of Ancient Fabrics Demolished

To the south of the Tolomato district which is bounded on the east by the street of that name is a piece of ground extending through from the street to Maria Sanchez Creek called Old Powder House lot. On this tract fifty years ago were some well grown sweet orange trees, and until the last three years had stood a one story house having two rooms. The easternmost was with a window on the north, and another on the south side: on the front, with a window on each side, was an old double door turning on several pairs of staples. It had evidently not all been built at once and may have gone from a powder house to a dwelling and taken as the addition a Spanish kitchen with clumsy chimney and huge fireplace. I have never known its history and the only name I have ever heard for the ground is Old Powder House Lot. Three years ago it was torn down, the stone beaten up and the shell thrown into a walk.

Scarcely less to be regretted has been the demolishing about the same time of the new Powderhouse which stood not far north of the redoubt El Poso southward of St. Francis Barracks. The edifice was in the nature of a parallelogram of thick wall, with a terrace surrounded by a high stone enclosure each of the corners terminating in a massive *cubo* or sentry box. The whole was of stone, sound and entire. It was said to have been built in consequence of the moisture of the Castle. Originally it was covered with tiles, which on the decay of the rafters were replaced in an unsightly manner by shingles and these were burned. A guard house in the front of stone and tiles had been destroyed some years before.

The English Church, the remains of which I have before spoken of, and the great barrack in the southern part of the town of which four great sticks of chimneys were standing when I came to the country, have four fireplaces to a side, and are the only buildings I believe that were erected by the English in the time of their stay, a period I have heard of over twenty years. I judge from this circumstance that the Spaniards must have left houses in plenty, and I remember seeing many walls standing for dwellings that had gone to decay or been burned, or perhaps had never been completed. To me the houses all appeared to be Spanish, and a few of them new.

The city was held by a formidable force. The Civil Governor Don Jose Coppinger,[31] was brigadier general in command. We have heard a little story of his knowledge of men that may be worth remembering. On coming to this country he was told of very great difficulty in getting good servants. He said that he had the solution to removing every obstacle. Having sought among the best that were recommended to him, he bought two for their capabilities, a man and a woman, told them what their cost had been, what would be the insurance on their lives and the interest on both sums. Their wages at the current rates would pay for all stated dates, when, if they had proved attentive and faithful they should be emancipated. The close of their servitude having come about near the same period, he called them to him, and agreeably to his promise gave them their free papers without any abatement. He expressed his many obligations for their industry, sobriety and entire faithfulness. The blacks desired to remain, even though without remuneration their terms of servitude had been so honored and happy. The governor was dissatisfied that they should continue and directed his major domo to see to the exact payment of their wages holding nature best served where gratitude and honor are not permitted to wander far from what may be of necessity.

Two companies from the second regiment of Cuba occupied the Castle and a company of mounted men where the school house for blacks has lately been permitted to be built (Old Powder House Lot) and thence called the Dragoon Lot.

The present Court House was the Post for a company of artillery.[32] Two companies of negroes were stationed in the convent of San Francisco and kept guard at the southern redoubt near El Poso. These blacks were distinguished for their good conduct and subordination. Their captains, two educated black gentlemen were often at our house, came sometimes to our store.

One of them, I remember, taught us the art of bleaching wax. The spiritual attendants on the soldiery were two Franciscan friars. They wore blue robes, sandals and very broad brimmed hats.

Subsequently, two regiments were sent from Spain, one belonging to a Catalan, the other to a Malaga regiment. The Cuban soldiers were aged and inferior, to those recently arrived, the finest looking body of men I ever saw. They had been in the wars against Napoleon and bore honorable scars. The town was well overawed before they had been in it for a year. They came to such excess at last that a soldier showed his insolence one Sunday morning at mass by taking the governor's unoccupied armchair, which stood at the right hand of the aisle of the church, formed by a double row of benches whereon the male part of the congregation sat. A part of the men finally mutinied one night, and sent a message by one of their number to the Governor who was found in the Castle, and they going out the City-gate, left the Province.

Appearance of the Neighborhoods of the Town

Looking to the southward of the city across the Bay about two miles distant might be seen a Spanish stone cottage among trees, a date tree, the only one in the country rising among them to an altitude of 80 feet, presenting the appearance of coming through the roof. This charming seat of Fish's Island, a part of Anastasia Island, divided from it by a little creek was planted by an American gentleman a long time before, from whom the islet received its name.[33] He was killed by lightning while on horseback, as I have heard people say.[34] His gravestone is among the orange trees. The widow remained there to live many years.

Opposite the town near the landing on what is called Quarry Creek that leads directly to a road to the Light House, had once been a house and there still the remains of a small orchard of different trees. To the northward near the extremity of the island among the last clump of trees springing from an elevation thrown up by Oglethorpe, is where the General coming from Georgia raised a battery attempting to reduce St. Augustine by siege.[35] Two shot holes made by a cannon he trained there are to be seen on the eastern wall of Castle San Marcos. Over all of those fields north of the City Lines were only a few palmetto camps, shelters from the dews and the sun's rays for those who there cultivated sweet potatoes and corn, a distance of fifteen hundred yards that were kept bare of house and tree for the free play of cannon, should occasion require, from the Castle. Then as now, the Indian tackey—*jaca*[36]—went to the island of Comacho [37] to eat salt grass and return with the rise of the water on the half tide: at evening the curlews flew rapidly east with loud calls along the City Lines to their resting places about the dark green jungles on Anastasia among the marshes of rasset—*zacate*[38]—had become parti-colored blue and white by the roosting upon them of the herons and cranes. In summer the roseat spoonbill crane was seen occasionally in pairs upon the shell bluffs of secluded channels and creeks and there strolled in half-furtive flights . . . the salt plains about the head of Tolomato in North River and crossed the San Pablo Creek and the San Juan River.

Some colonists introduced by the English about fifty years ago, chiefly from the Island of Minorca occupied the land in fields that stretch from the Gates to the woods called Mil y Quinte, the distance of 1000 yards.[39]

Of the Manner & Condition of the Town

The houses in which the better sort of people resided, persons for the most part in the civil and military service, were built of coquina, the shell stone cut from the ancient quarries of Anastasia.[40] Many were flat roofed, perhaps many had originally been so, the walls plastered and kept clean with lime wash made from burned oyster shells. The ground floors were universally *tabi*.[41] The northern part of the city was called Minorcan town by those who spoke English.

The roofs of the houses in many instances were thatched with the palmetto, and some were altogether covered with those leaves. The quarter to the westward upon which the wild begins, beginning at the Catholic burial ground, was an open field called Tolomato.

The "Picolato Avenue" was not open then,[42] and the Maria Sanchez Creek was crossed where the northern causeway is over it now by a little wooden bridge that led to a large orange grove. This is the only street that has been opened within the ancient limits in my time. The Southern street, a continuation of Treasury Lane near which I work with my hoe has been obliterated. The part of the avenue called King St. (for what reason I do not know) was enlarged from an alley about 30 years ago, by taking land into it from the lot belonging to the government on the north side. The avenue next south, which passes the Maria Sanchez Creek by a plank bridge in a causeway of coquina was built by Spain. This was the road from the forest into town over the San Sebastian creek crossed by a wooden bridge built more recently by the English and there are some vestiges of it remaining on the western shore.

The market place for meat was at the Plaza in the side of the present market house on the eastern end of a low, one story latticed building. At the western end was raised a bell, in the two intermediate rooms were the material belonging to the King's launch that gave pilotage across the bar. To the south of this end was a single building called La Botica, which was the shop of the King's apothecary. To the south and east on the angle formed between these two buildings was the vegetable and fruit market. Beef and pork were the meats of the market. Cattle were never stall fed. The governor had a flock of sheep and we also made trial of a considerable number. Tho they bred well, they were so worried by dogs that no advantage came of them.

Fish ever in plenty and cheap was sold on little tables about 4 ft. square and vegetables were in greater quantity and perfection than I have ever seen them since. The *chiote*, of the size and shape of a pear and ribbed like a melon, commonly grew on arbors. The *tania* or *vio* was often in the market baskets.[43] The tomato was then eaten, and the sweet pepper roasted, skinned and covered with oil was a favorite dish. Fruit was generally sold from the basket carried about the streets on the head. In this manner shrimp were disposed of at six cents a plate; oysters at the same price the quartful; stone crabs taken among the coquina rocks on the south beach or brought from Matanzas, figs, grapes, peaches and oranges, honey in the comb, all in abundance.

It is worthy of reflexion[*sic*] how small has been the addition to the fruits and vegetables that were grown here by the Spaniards. Although the trees, shrubs and plants introduced since the cession of the Province have been numerous both from the cooler and the milder latitudes, I find but two in my memory that are attended with a promise of success. These are the *cimaron*, or wild banana brought as I hear from New Orleans by Kingsley Beatty Gibbs, and the loquat seed from the same place first planted by William Pacetti.[44] In a word, the soil has proved too arid on the one side or the climate on the other too cold. So after these many experiences and having in mind those made in previous ages when the inhabitants were in constant intercourse with the Antilles and Mexico, one would rather lean to the opinion that nothing is likely to be cultivated here that has not already been brought, unless it come from some distant region. These words are not spoken to discourage, but for attentive reflection, yet desirable varieties of both fruit and vegetables may be found and added to those already in cultivation.

Two sorts of figs, the black and the white, were growing here at the time of the cession. The brown Ischia variety, called here Smyrna, was brought here by O'Connor about 35 years ago.[45] The mammoth variety came afterward. The yam was the only variety of sweet potato in cultivation, the early white with red heel, the yellow and brimstone kinds, that now appear to have run out, were introduced from Georgia shortly after our arrival in this country. The large white sort was brought here later by Zephaniah Kingsley from Haiti. The root was grabbled, and not dug. Of the grapes there was the common black variety of today, and occasionally a white vine, that came from the Malaga grape or raisin. A smaller black has been introduced, the Isabella, and the scuppernong. Other kinds requiring rich sustenance have disappeared. Within a few years, the Tangerine has been brought here by Dr. Oliver Bronson grafted on a lemon stock, and the propagation has also been by seed and bud.[46]

The Spanish pink, which I have never seen growing on the ground is as cherished now as formerly never having been permitted to die out, and still remaining the ornament of the balconies. This pink is smaller than the carnation, is streaked and besides being more spicy has the peculiarity of always keeping the cup unbroken. The tradition is that the flower came from Havana.

Of the Outer & Interior Commerce

The commerce of St. Augustine, the only town or settlement on the peninsula was principally with Havana. From there came from time to time the pay of the civil and military service, and in a good degree the provisions and clothing that were consumed. From there were brought *judias*,[47] black beans, garbanzas, chickpeas, dried Veracruz peppers for soup, saffron for tinting it, sugar, sweetments, wines, rum, olive oil, linens and in general the fine stuffs and materials used in that climate for female attire. With them continually arrived the delicate fruit of the tropics.

The government, not unmindful of this opportunity occasionally supplied wants that looking to other sources might not have been satisfied, and sought to make up the return cargoes, among which were the trapped cardinal and the *trinzonetti*, mocking bird, reared from the nest in the Spring previous in spacious palmetto cane cages, and educated in the Spanish airs.

The Indians frequented the town from the interior, for exchange they brought ponys, hogs, occasionally a slave, beeswax, wild honey, snakeroot, bear's oil, raw and dressed deer skins. By the Indians, the public want of venison and wild turkey was well provided. They took back with them in their packs, powder, lead, blue-checked cotton homespun, shrouds, a few milk-white and blue beads, now and then a pocket looking-glass, a comb, worsted binding, blue, red and yellow, with a little carmine for the face to be used on festive occasions. Some who lingered late about the town brought back loads of dry sticks to sell for fuel and in their season, huckleberries and the fruit of the palmetto of which white natives like themselves were very fond.[48]

The *Barbarita* conveying money here at the appointed times for the payment of troops and merchandize as well as men was constantly in movement, her arrival and departure being the continual subject of the public rejoicing and solicitude.[49]

An important source of support to the residents of the town at that time was the orange grove. I have known a half a dozen American vessels to be in port at the same time, receiving and unloading. Lying out in the stream, the cargoes were lightered to shore, and carried in wheel-barrows or rolled on the ground to the Custom House, standing two doors from the corner on the western side of the street that goes northward from the City Basin. They brought soap, flour, tobacco in leaf, blue homespuns, for which they got in exchange principally oranges, reckoned at fifty cents a hundred, taking them to ports along the coast, from Charleston to New Haven. The fruit at that time was gathered in October and November when it had reached its full size and was becoming yellow. On this occasion oranges carried better, the trees were healthier and bore more regularly than they do now when the practice is opposite. The yards in the town were filled with the trees and the tongue of land between the creeks was a succession of groves a long way down, which were completely destroyed in the Spring of 1835.[50]

The Inhabitants Their Dress and Amusements

The population appears to be at that time more numerous than it has been since. Some blacks who fled from their masters in the United States as free, raised crops for the most part of corn, cowpeas, melons and pumpkins on different tracts out of town where they thought themselves safe, and some white families of English remained with their descendants as Cultivators. Horatio S. Dexter, who had a plantation on the San Juan river which is called Volusia, and his wife were the first Americans here. After we had come, they brought their children from Rhode Island.[51]

The men in the common way wore hunting shirts of chequed cotton; palmetto hats for the most part from Havana, and *moggasins*. The women wore the silk and lace *manton* on going out with a silk slip, shoes of cloth or on festive occasions, of satin made by themselves. The only bonnet in town was a beaver.

At early mass a white lace veil covered the head and bosom of the lady, and the black lace later in the day. Parasols came afterwards. At church, tags and ribbons fluttered from the candelabra, incense arose before the altar, then from a silver censor; music vocal and instrumental proceeded from the gallery, and the women seated on their several rugs upon the *tabi* floor counted their rosaries in prayer, and flashed their tasseled fans. On Sundays after the devotions of the morning the inhabitants were free to pass the remaining hours in amusements, and many were the days in the calendar for celebration and public festivity. The bank of oyster shell, on which Fort Moosa stands, was a favorite spot for entertainments for the gathering of the town, the people riding thither on tackeys of a Sunday afternoon. Brushwood was brought together the day before by a negro with a canoe-load of oysters. These, collected about in heaps, were roasted and seasoned with oil, orange juice and *ojo* [garlic], the people made merry with Catalan wine, and smoking cigars. The little cost and sobriety of these entertainments would astonish now.

The people were the gayest I can imagine. Serenades, processions, balls, picnics they called "*convites*," masquerades, came the year round in constant succession. The youths too had their amusements, marbles, tops and kites. On St. John's day in June, commenced the recreation of sea bathing. [For St. John's day] three days, preceded by many evenings of carnival, were passed in Masking in the streets.

There were no vehicles other than the beef carts that are still to be seen, except a single one-horse chaise, the property of the king's treasurer. Lamps were not in use and the common utensils were so rare that some iron pots we imported were taken from us before they could reach the Custom House. We introduced four-wheeled carriages and Jersey wagons, brought from New York. With them a line of passengers was attempted to be run to meet a row boat at the mouth of Pablo Creek coming from the St. Marys. It was the route of the only post and mounted dragoon who took and brought the mail once a week.

Changes in the Ancient City have gone on slowly and steadily, not in its edifices more than in the manners of its inhabitants, but in nothing have men changed since the time I have spoken as in the way of thought. I am no less sensible of the changes that have come over me.

The . . . [illegible] . . . of papers that have been run over for me, admonishes that there is a time when I should draw to a close. I return to speak of myself. I have little knowledge beyond my intercourse with men and what my experience teaches. The labors of my mature life have been confined to this field and these trees. For the long period of 50 years I have not worked out of them a single summer, except in the three years and a week I was out of town during the civil war, which I account the better part of my life.[52]

I can read. While in Connecticut my mistress taught me my letters and to spell as far as "baker," but I went no further until I came to live in St. Augustine. Here I applied to my young master to teach me. He consented and said that after I learned to read one lesson well I might learn all the rest by myself that I desired to know. So he taught me the hymn "when I can read my title clear."[53] My obligations for the aid will not appear immoderate, when it is known that not a great many years before I had given him his first knowledge of the alphabet. In the course of time I associated with Caleb, a Presbyterian black and we read together chapter and chapter. From him, with a good memory I learned much.[54] Judge E. B. Gould whom some can remember still, of the same church, taught privately, colored people who desired to learn and I acquired of him lessons in the spelling book.[55]

When I was 16 years, or thereabouts, I had some religious feeling but lost them on coming to live among the Spaniards. I had asked myself "Why can I not go to heaven?" "I do not swear, I do not steal, I keep no bad company." I retired into the bush and prayed. I read something. The first religious instruction that I received was in the year 1823 from Mr. Glen, a Methodist minister and on the 26 of December, I joined the church and took the sacrament. Our first and only meetinghouse was built on land given by Mr. Burroughs and Mr. Carr, where I have exhorted my brethren from the time of the Mexican War when it was built, though in truth the license to preach did not issue to me until 1867 and that to be a preacher in the last year. My ministry covers a period of 40 years.

Within the scope of my vision there is little in the vegetable form that was living when I came here. Age, the borer, the affix, the frost, have in their time and season done their several work. The avenue of orange trees are but sprouts of the trees that came from the seeds planted 46 or 47 years ago, once destroyed by frost and subsequently for many years kept down by insects. A hedge to the southwest of it on the confine of a neighbor's ground is of a date still earlier. The two black fig trees were young trees three years old when I set them out 42 years ago. The *seringa* was introduced from Charleston in 1820.[56] The two standing there of lilac with a girth of trunk of 12 inches and a height of nearly 60 feet were blooming 37 years since. The mulberries about the dwelling doubtless from the forest, certainly attained great dimensions were originally nine, of which two have been destroyed by . . . [The manuscript ends here in the middle of a sentence.]

Notes

1. The translator of this prayer represented by the initials A. J. C. was not identified.

2. Probably the Moria.

3. *Voandzeia subterranea*, the Bambarra groundnut, similar to peanuts (Gibbs 1965:124).

4. The Spanish word *ufa* is translated as "parasitically" (Gooch and Paredes 1978:583), thus by extension in this context meaning as a passenger on a horse.

5. This side note may refer to tattooing or scarification of the body to mark group membership.

6. The Fulah (a.k.a. Fula, Fulbe, Falani, Filani) were seminomadic cattle raisers, usually Muslim in religion.

7. Several towns in West Africa are named after the Bambara group, a Manding subgroup.

8. Immediately northeast of the Rio Pongo delta is a town called Kissing.

9. Taylor, the owner of the slave factory, has not been definitely identified.

10. Jephaniah Kingsley, owner of a sizable plantation in East Florida, also maintained a trading station on the African coast in Senegal. John Frazer, owner of a plantation in northeast Florida, also maintained a trading station at the Rio Pongo in West Africa.

11. The Juluf is probably a misspelling of Jolof, a group that is part of the Wolof who lived south of Senegal and the Rio Gambia, which is north of the Rio Pongo region.

12. Captain Brown was the master of the brig *Sally*.

13. The merchant was Josiah Smith.

14. Buckingham Smith, born October 31, 1810.

15. The embargo occurred during the War of 1812.

16. Sir George Cockburn, British Admiral, was assigned to the Georgia/Florida border area during the War of 1812.

17. Anita Amelia Smith (Porter), Buckingham Smith's sister, born in 1815.

18. The island referred to is Anastasia Island opposite the city of St. Augustine.

19. Castillo de San Marcos, built by the Spanish in 1687 to guard St. Augustine. The narrator used the English translation, "Castle," in further references throughout the manuscript.

20. Now known as Fort Matanzas National Monument.

21. Present-day St. Johns River.

22. The proper designation for this fort is Gracia Real de Santa Teresa de Mose. In 1738, the Spanish authorities established a sanctuary town to shelter escaped slaves from Georgia and the Carolinas, who then became free. A fort was built called Fort Mose or the "Negro Fort."

23. Fr. Michael Crosby, a secular priest who was educated in Spain, came to St. Augustine in 1791 and served until his death in 1822, just as the American Period was beginning (Gannon 1965:102,122).

24. This building still stands and is referred to today as "The Treasurer's House" or "The Pena-Peck House."

25. The Constitution Monument, as it is now called, still stands in the middle of the central plaza. It was erected in 1812–1813 in honor of the short-lived republican government in Spain. Soon after it was erected, a royal order called for all such monuments to be demolished, so this monument is a rare example. The square and compass mentioned here are Masonic symbols.

26. The church still stands in the same location. It was later referred to as the St. Augustine Cathedral and is now the Cathedral Basilica of St. Augustine.

27. The building was originally the Bishop's House (Palacio Episcopal) built in the First Spanish period. It was later used by the British as a barracks, then for a short time as a church, and subsequently renovated to serve as Council House and Assembly rooms. It fell into disuse during the Second Spanish period (Gordon 2002:103–104).

28. Enrique White arrived in 1796 to become governor of East Florida after previously serving as governor of West Florida in Pensacola. He died in office and a pile of stones, *majonera*, marked his grave in Tolomato cemetery.

29. This building, still standing, was first the headquarters of the Franciscans serving the Florida missions and was later used as a military barracks for many years. Today, it is the administrative headquarters of the Florida Army National Guard.

30. The Jesuit fathers founded this "church," known as "Nombre de Dios," as a mission to the Indians in 1565. It was the first of the Florida missions and its grounds are preserved today by the Catholic Church (Gannon 1965:27).

31. Jose Maria Coppinger was the able and dignified last colonial governor of Florida.

32. The courthouse was on Artillery Lane just west of Aviles Street. The building is no longer in existence.

33. Jesse Fish, originally from New York, resided in the St. Augustine area during three periods of its history. The plantation that he claimed on Anastasia Island was approximately ten-thousand acres. His was the first extensive orange grove in Florida.

34. The narrator was incorrect. The man killed by lightning was the son of Jesse Fish, Sr.

35. Governor James Edward Oglethorpe of Georgia led a raid against St. Augustine by land and sea in 1740. The narrator is referring to the batteries thrown up on Anastasia Island to fire cannons at the town. The siege failed.

36. Indian tackeys were semiwild horses common in the St. Augustine area even as late as the turn of the twentieth century. The Spanish word *jaca* refers to a thick-set, short-legged horse or pony.

37. Now called Camachee Island, it is situated southeast of St. Augustine on the Intracoastal Waterway.

38. Rasset and *zacate* are marsh grasses; hay or fodder.

39. The Minorcans were a large group of Mediterraneans brought to Florida in 1768 as indentured servants to farm an indigo plantation. After nine years, they were given sanctuary in St. Augustine where many of their descendents still live.

40. Coquina is a local shellstone formed during the Pleistocene era, composed mostly of small marine clam shells of the genus *Donax*. Coquina was used extensively as building material in colonial St. Augustine.

41. Tabby (the English spelling) is a concrete composed of equal parts of lime, sand, and shell. In St. Augustine, coarse oyster shell was used for rough work, such as walls; coquina was usually the shell component of tabby floors (Manucy 1962:164).

42. Now called King Street.

43. Both *tania* and *vio* are tropical plants of the *Xanthosoma* family, related to the

elephant ear plant. The roots are edible, similar to *taro*. They were first imported into St. Augustine from the West Indies (Taylor 1936:882).

44. Kingsley Beatty Gibbs inherited the plantation of his uncle, Jephaniah Kingsley, on Fort George Island in extreme northeast Florida. William Pacetti was a descendant of the Minorcan colony of 1768.

45. Probably a ship captain.

46. Dr. Oliver Bronson, a medical doctor, was a friend of Buckingham Smith and executor of Smith's will. He precipitated the formation of the Buckingham Smith Benevolent Association with the mission of care for aged Negroes in St. Augustine.

47. *Judias*, imported from Vera Cruz, are peppers used for soup.

48. The fruit of the palmetto most likely refers to the hearts of palm, the cabbage-like head at the base of the leaves. The berries, on the other hand, are virtually inedible, although they were a food resource for the Ais Indians and others near Cape Canaveral.

49. The *Barbarita* was one of the last ships in the Second Spanish period that carried the *situado* to St. Augustine. St. Augustine was never self-supporting in Spanish times, necessitating that royal funds and supplies be sent yearly in a ship(s) from Cuba to the Florida presidio (Bushnell 1994:43–48).

50. After many years of mild weather, the worst freeze in the recorded history of St. Augustine hit the town in 1835. The extreme cold caused severe damage to the orange groves.

51. Horatio Dexter founded the town of Volusia as part of his plantation enterprise on the St. Johns River. Lake Dexter is named after him. The narrator surprisingly singles out Dexter and his family for mention. The Dexters were likely friends of the Smith family.

52. Jack Smith stayed in New York with Buckingham Smith through the turbulent times of the Civil War.

53. This hymn was written by Isaac Watts, the famous English hymn writer of the eighteenth century, and set to music by William Mather (Housewright 1991:317–318).

54. Caleb was a slave whose owner was Dr. William H. Simmons, prominent citizen of St. Augustine. Dr. Simmons was described as a strong booster of St. Augustine who attempted to have the town continued as the capital of Florida in the American Period. Nevertheless, he bowed to the majority and was one of the two men who eventually selected the site of Tallahassee for the state Capital (Graham 1978:33,56–58).

55. E. B. Gould was a newspaper editor and staunch Presbyterian.

56. *Serenga* is probably *Heavea brasiliensis*, commonly called *seringia*, which is a rubber plant.

2

Slave and Master

In 1875, the second article of a two-part series appeared in *Harpers New Monthly Magazine*. The article, entitled "The Ancient City" by Constance Fenimore Woolson, dedicated considerable space to the former slave, "Uncle Jack." One illustration showed him approaching his cabin leaning on a cane with a hoe thrust over his shoulder and another sketch showed him in his proper Methodist minister clothes. After a description of his cabin and remarks about his venerable age and the delights of a visit with him in his orange grove, the reader was informed that "Before the war his master sent him several times to Boston with large sums of money, and intrusted [*sic*] him with important business, which he never failed to execute properly" (Woolson 1875:169).

Whether this statement was actually the truth or hyperbole to impress the reader, Ms. Woolson gave a nineteenth-century picture of a trusted slave in service to his master. Nevertheless, the anecdote does represent Jack Smith—formerly Sitiki—as an unusual slave, and the relationship between him and his master, Buckingham Smith, as equally unusual. From the distance of a century and a half, accurate evaluation of their association is problematic. However, clues in the narrative and other sources are illuminating.

The evolution of their relationship from enslavement to employment to collaboration was partly a consequence of their age difference. Jack was born a decade or more before Buckingham and outlived him by as much. In the beginning years, Jack occupied a status position as the older man guiding the young Smith boy. As Buckingham grew older, the relationship gradually realigned and Jack's status as a slave beholden to his master emerged. Ultimately, Buckingham became a well-respected man of the world, while Jack modestly refers to his fifty years with the hoe in the Smith's orange grove. That self-assessment belies Jack's trusted position within the Smith family as well as his actual stature as a minister, advisor, and adjudicator within the black community. As old age approached both men, their relationship realigned again, but one hesitates to label it.

Both of these men were atypical individuals for their time, even to the point of being what might now be referred to as "characters." The painting of Buckingham at the age of eight as a proper little rich boy contrasts sharply with a photograph of him after the Civil War, showing a slightly disheveled gentleman with his tie askew. Even more telling is the comment contained in a letter that Andrew Anderson wrote to his mother from New York advising her, "Buck Smith is going South in the next steamer. He looks as wild & talks as wise as ever—However savage his appearance, you must not be afraid of him for he is perfectly harmless." She was likely to encounter him as the Anderson orange grove was by then just south of the Smith property in St. Augustine (Graham 1978:143). Fifty years later, reminiscing to a friend, Anderson wrote: "He [Buckingham] was, as I remember him, a peculiar man, but one whose opinions were highly respected by his friends" (Anderson to Ransom, Letter, 1923). Likewise, Jack was described after his death as having been "one of the curiosities of St. Augustine" (Webb 1885:185).

Both were unique in their own way. Buckingham Smith is still considered the first prominent Spanish Borderlands scholar of the eastern United States. Jack Smith, as time went on, was one of the few African-born blacks in St. Augustine, and certainly considered the only one of major stature in the community. Both arrived at their ultimate achievement largely through their own efforts and perseverance. Jack's career, in some ways, was the more remarkable, as he had neither Buckingham's family status nor the freedom for an initial boost.

Photograph of a portrait of Buckingham Smith as a proper little rich
boy at the age of eight, 1819. Photographic Collection, St. Augustine
Historical Society. By permission of St. Augustine Historical Society,
St. Augustine, Florida.

Jack is usually spoken of as Buckingham's slave, but a look at the record
reveals that Buckingham was actually Jack's owner for only four or five
years. The length of time is uncertain because the documents lack clarity regarding the status of emancipation at both national and state levels,
as well as where Jack was at the time. After Buckingham's father, Josiah
Smith, bought Jack in 1808, he was Jack's master for seventeen years until
Josiah's death in 1825. Hannah, Josiah's widow, then inherited Jack and the
other slaves. Hannah was Jack's owner for the longest period—thirty-three
years—until her death in 1858. At that time, Buckingham, the sole surviv-
ing member of his immediate family, bought Jack and the other slaves from
his mother's estate. The end of the Civil War brought a definitive end to

Photograph circa 1860 of Buckingham Smith—note the careless tie.
Photographic Collection, St. Augustine Historical Society. By permission
of St. Augustine Historical Society, St. Augustine, Florida.

Jack's servitude, but he remained on the Smith estate, probably because of
his advanced age as he was approaching seventy.

In spite of his short tenure as master, Buckingham, as the ranking white
male in the family and for some years his mother's lawyer, had a controlling
hand in the supervision of Jack and the other slaves. Buckingham continued
to trust in Jack's integrity, which was a hallmark of the Smiths' attitude. That
trust was reinforced by Jack remaining with the Smith family after he was
captured by the British in the War of 1812 and offered his liberty, although
we can never be sure as to how much coercion was present in this incident.
The possibility that Jack was under strong pressure to remain as an enslaved
person must be considered.

As slaveholders, the Smiths behaved responsibly and ethically for their
era. The remarkable longevity of the Smith slaves shows care and concern

through the years and responsible medical care is documented in the records. For example, one page from Dr. Seth Peck's ledger from 1845 lists
care for the white family members as well as medical attention for three
slaves. The bill listed for Jack and two other slaves was $15.35, a large sum at
that time when some laborers earned only five dollars for a month's work
(PFP 1845). Expenditures on behalf of slave health were as much or more
for economic as humanitarian reasons, considering the monetary value of
healthy slaves as working property. The Smith family was affluent enough
to afford the investment.

Reasons exist to believe that Buckingham supported Jack's effort to become a Methodist minister. When the Methodist congregation was at low
ebb after 1845, Jack mounted a campaign to build a decent church and one of
Buckingham's good friends, Burroughs Carr, donated the land for the building. Probably other of Buckingham's friends and acquaintances subscribed
to the building fund as well, which would have added to the meager funds
donated by the congregation, most of whom were slaves. No other black congregation worshipped in its own church building during subsequent years, as
demonstrated by various maps of the town drawn between 1845 and 1865.

Another factor contributed to Jack's unusual relationship with Buckingham. Slaves were ranked in St. Augustine—as they were elsewhere in urban
communities in the South—by the rank of the owner. Buckingham Smith
enjoyed high regard in the town and in Florida, judging by the elected and
appointed positions that he held in the city and state. His eminence as a
scholar extended his influence to other parts of the nation, particularly New
York and Washington. Even long after slavery was abolished, blacks in urban locations such as St. Augustine mentioned as a matter of pride the well-
known men or families for whom they worked. This kind of pecking order
in parallel black and white status was remarked on as late as the end of the
twentieth century in St. Augustine (Griffin and Edwards 1990). Certainly,
the affiliation with Buckingham and his attendant status was an operative
factor in Jack's life, notwithstanding his own successful life.

Two special projects engaged Buckingham's and Jack's time together:
cultivation of the splendid orange grove and Buckingham's transcription of
Jack's narrative. The narrative was a kind of life review for both as well as
a nostalgic look at St. Augustine in colonial times. Buckingham wrote his

last will and testament near the time when "The Story of Uncle Jack" was being revised, and, not surprisingly, Jack is listed as a prominent legatee and, significantly, is mentioned first in the document. (See Appendix D, "Buckingham Smith's Last Will and Testament.")

What can one say about the two men—a slave and his master—whose lives were closely meshed for much of the nineteenth century? Probably each knew the other better in some ways than members of their own race knew them. They had long ago adjusted to each other's ways, the differences smoothed by constant association. Long-time mutual understanding and work together furnished an important bond, yet the difference in status between the two men always existed as a fact of life. Never were they considered equals. As far as their personalities were concerned, Buckingham seems to have been the more volatile. Jack was the steadying influence, and very dignified apparently, although he practiced his religion with "zeal," as his obituary noted. Friendship is too strong a word, but certainly there was some mutual confidence between them.

II

LIFE IN AFRICA

3

Life Before Captivity

The description given at the beginning of the foregoing narrative is dramatic. We can easily imagine a small boy living more than two hundred years ago with his Muslim family in the safety of a clay-walled town in an interior section of West Africa. We soon find out that he is fated to become an enslaved world traveler, forced into that role by events beyond his control. Who was he and where did he come from? Some of the answers we know, while in other cases we must guess.

The narrative account and the words remembered of his language fail to yield an exact location of the town where Sitiki was born. Describing the land, he indicates, "the country I was born in was everywhere stony. Some portions were mountainous and in parts water came in rivulets & fell in cascades." Working with this information and other clues, it can be surmised that Sitiki was born on the east side of the Futa Jalon mountain range where the mountain chain verges on the broad savannah of the Western Sudan.

Linguistic analysis of the words Sitiki gave from his original language supports this location. He said that he was "born in an interior country of western Africa" and that he spoke "Guinea." After going through a chain of linguists, Valentin Vydrine, the noted linguist of West Africa in the eighteenth and nineteenth centuries, was reached. According to him, Sitiki's tongue cannot be identified with any modern African language: "It has some similarities with West Manding languages, some similarities with Mokole languages (especially Koranko and Kakabe). . . . It is probable that it was one of smaller Futa Jallon Mande languages of the Mokole group that disappeared under the theocratic power of the Fulbe. We should also keep in mind that the linguistic geography of Futa Jallon is still understudied . . . ."[1] (See Appendix C, "Analysis of Sitiki's Language.")

The Fulbe (Fula), who were mainly Muslim pastoralists, were attempting to conquer many other groups in West Africa during Sitiki's time there. They might have succeeded, given their mobility on horseback, but for the increasing European incursions into West Africa in the early nineteenth century (Brooks, G. E. 1998:155). These nomadic Muslims did, however, wipe out or subsume some groups.

Sitiki's town of origin may have been east of Labe, a large market town known at that time as a center of the textile and salt trades. Labe was at a crossroads of two trade routes. The direct route reached the West African coast at the Rio Nunez, while another indirect route reached the Rio Pongo delta to the south. Either route may have been near where Sitiki was eventually transshipped to the Americas.

Speaking of his own town, he mentioned salt being "brought to the town on asses in great pieces." Salt, slaves, metals, palm oil, textiles, and other items were the major exports and internal trade items at the time. Nevertheless, the possibility that Sitiki's birthplace was somewhat farther to the east or south than the Labe area cannot be ruled out.

A small town near Timbo is another likely birthplace for Sitiki. Trade routes at Timbo reached the coast at the Rio Pongo or farther south near Moria. This section of West Africa, east of the Futa Jalon mountains, was composed of fields and broad grazing areas interrupted by deeply folded mountains. Small villages were occasionally interspersed by market towns. Such a town with monotonously dust-colored houses and public buildings may have been what Sitiki called home.

Like his town of origin, Sitiki's birth date is also a matter of speculation. He remembers that he was four or five years old at the time of his capture. The first date that we have is 1807, the year of his arrival in Charleston, South Carolina, at which time he speaks of himself as "at play," which may be an indication that he was not yet past early adolescence. Later in St. Augustine,

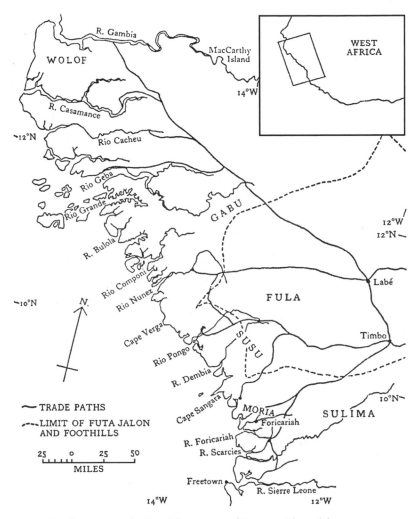

Trade routes in the Futa Jalon region of Guinea. Adapted from map
in Ph.D. dissertation of Bruce Mouser, 1971. By permission of Bruce Mouser,
La Crosse, Wisconsin.

a property document listing the enslaved persons of his owner, Josiah Smith,
noted Jack as twenty-one years old in 1817. In contrast, a handwritten diary
of Joshua Nichols Glenn, who converted Jack to Methodism in 1824, notes
him as thirty years old. These two source documents then indicate a birth
date of either 1794 or 1796.

Census data later in his life are conflicting also, to say the least, although
general indications are that he was born in the middle 1790s. Reports of Jack's

age at death vary widely. His 1882 obituary in the local St. Augustine news-paper reported his age as 105 years. Elsewhere it was reported that he died at the age of 110 (Webb 1885:185). The burial permit, also filed in 1882, recorded Jack as ninety-five years of age at death, which is also questionable, particu-larly since the doctors who signed these documents often relied on hearsay for noting age at death for older black individuals. Census data likewise were conflicting. The 1880 census—the last in which he appeared—listed his age as ninety years (U.S. Census 1880). Jack was probably eighty-nine to ninety years old at the time of his death. Advanced age, exceedingly uncommon in the nineteenth century, was noteworthy. Hence, exaggeration of age often occurred, especially for slaves whose birth dates were unknown.

We must also speculate on the religious life in Sitiki's town of origin. Some African towns were completely pagan and others were Muslim, while still others maintained elements of both religions. In reality, the newer Mus-lim religion grafted onto the pagan base showed elements of both forms of worship, as is common when two religions meet. Since Sitiki remembered no house of worship, perhaps Muslims were a minority in the town, unless this perceived absence was an artifact of his young age. Bringing a third reli-gion into the mix, Christian missionaries began proselytizing in West Africa about the time that Sitiki left.

We know that Sitiki's family followed the ways of Islam, as he remembers his father kneeling at prayer on a sheepskin rug with his head touching the earth. The childhood memory of the words of the prayer—"Ala-ala-mama-lay-sutta"—is interpreted as a rendition of the daily prayer of Islam recited by the devout five times a day. For clarity in the narrative, this prayer is trans-lated into English somewhat loosely as "there is no deity but the deity and Mohammed [is] the envoy of God."

The names of Sitiki's family are puzzling. The father's name (Deva) and the mother's name (Jene) are not of Muslim derivation, perhaps indicating that the parents' conversion to Islam occurred when they were adults. Sitiki did not remember his younger brother's name.

His own name, recorded as Sitiki, is probably a misspelling of Siddiq or al-Siddiq or Siddiqui. The name is not easily translated, but is variously rep-resented as friend, the blessed, sainted, of God, or blessed with honesty—honesty being a strong value in many West African cultures. When given to a child, the name is usually attached to the end of a longer name, often that of a celebrated person of Islam. An example of this is the name "Abu Bakr al-Sid-diq," a man whose slave narrative discloses that he was born in the Western Sudan, near the time that Sitiki was born (Wilks 1967:152–167). The revered Abu Bakr—for whom this contemporary of Sitiki's was named—was the Prophet Mohammed's close companion, father-in-law, and first successor. Siddiq was the ending name of many boys in Muslim families at that time, a practice that has survived into modern times. For so young a child as Sitiki was at the time of capture, he most likely remembered only part of his full name. In addition, Buckingham Smith in writing the name in the narrative must have spelled the name as he heard it.

Not yet old enough to attend the Muslim school, Sitiki observed the schoolboys writing on wooden tablets in a language that he did not know,

Photograph of modern West African Muslim boy near the same age as Sitiki when captured. Photographer John Isaac. By permission of John Isaac, Bronxville, New York.

which was likely Arabic. Muslim boys customarily began attending school at the age of six in order to learn Arabic, taught by the *ulama* [learned men]. Frequently, children under school age were taught at home by their grandmothers or at the knee of some other older woman in the extended kin group.

Male children in families of craftspeople began apprenticeship at an early age. Not surprisingly, Sitiki tells of watching his father practicing his trade. Deva was a weaver. In most West African societies, weavers occupied an intermediate position in the class structure, although there were exceptions. The elite were the rulers, holy men, headmen, and successful traders. Next, composing part of the incipient middle class, were the craftspeople. Beneath them in status, the lowest and poorest free groups in West Africa were the farmers, herdsmen, and soldiers, whose position was above the slaves.

Sitiki gives us thirteen words in his native language but also renders several of these in "Mandingo," an indication that he came to know that language as well as his own. Luckily for Sitiki, throughout most of his captivity in Africa, his local dialect was understandable to those around him. Never again after leaving Africa did he meet a person speaking his own language. One African whom Jack encountered thought Jack was speaking "Mora." Perhaps this reference was to Moria.

The remembered words indicate that his hearth language was a dialect of Mande. This assertion is partially confirmed by the fact that he gave the "Mandingo" translations for "fire" and "rice" as well as the corresponding words in his own language. Mandingo is a term popularly used to designate the trade language of the Western Sudan, generally a composite of the Mande languages.

In addition to his memory of blacksmith shops, saddle makers, tanning shops, soap makers, and gunpowder manufacturers, Sitiki particularly noticed the soldiers, as any boy might. The troops that Sitiki observed carried a variety of weapons from swords and spears to bows and arrows, while some even sported guns and rode horses. These horsemen were probably the nomadic Fulbe. If so, we might wonder if Sitiki observed small children of this group who often learned to ride and use a bow and arrow as early as the age of four.

The music that Sitiki heard was from soldiers who blew blasts on ivory horns, beat drums, and sang and played on various instruments—harps, banjos, and guitars. In traditional West African music, specific occasions called for certain musical instruments (McKissak and McKissak 1994:71–72). The coming of royalty was always announced by the *tabula*, a ceremonial drum, and by the *guimbris*, a guitar with only two strings. Another stringed instrument, the *bolon*, heralded war. Used for pleasure, the harp, called *Koro*, usually included twenty-seven strings.

In the narrative, Sitiki mentions an "instrument that looks like a piano," which might have been the small thumb-piano or hand-piano, an instrument widely used in Africa and later adapted for use in the Americas, particularly in the Caribbean. The instrument consisted of a little box or board with metal prongs, each producing a different note. Rather than a thumb-piano, the instrument might have been the *balaphon*, a type of xylophone made of wood blocks mounted on graduated gourds in a row (Roberts 1972:24–25).

Sitiki described the townspeople as being black and offers the opinion that their attire was similar to that of "our Indians." This reference is not to the earlier Timucua Indians in Florida but to the Seminole Indians who pushed into the area in the eighteenth century. Some clothing was imported from Scotland and sold to the Seminoles during the British Period of Florida's history and even later by British traders in the Second Spanish period. This attire may have had a vague resemblance to the dress of the townspeople seen in Africa. As to the women's dress in Africa, the only mention by Sitiki is of gold ornaments that marked their status in the community. His mother was so adorned, and later, when captured, the slavers immediately took her gold jewelry.

These wisps of early memory that Sitiki recorded were the selective memories of a young child. Yet, he brought forth a vivid picture of life in Africa in the late eighteenth century, which has some intrinsic historical value and also provides a base from which to examine his future life. Had he not been enslaved, fate would have most likely decreed that he become a respected weaver, such as his father, in one of the small towns of West Africa, living content as a free man and a Muslim with multiple wives and numerous children. Or, given the native intelligence evident in his subsequent life, he might even have become a learned African Muslim.

Note

1. Valentin Vydrine, Museum of Anthropology, University of Saint Petersburg, Russia, e-mail communication, April 29, 2005. (See Appendix C, "Analysis of Sitiki's Language," for full text.)

4

Capture and Enslavement

Capture and its ally kidnapping occupy a special place in the imagination, romantic and traumatic at the same time; a life torn from its base, never again to be the same. Sitiki was an African boy in the fourth or fifth year of his life when suddenly everything was wrenched away, transforming him into a virtual orphan.

In fifteen terse sentences, Sitiki recounted this hapless episode, a common one in eighteenth-century West Africa. Enslavement could occur in a number of ways: through wars; through an individual wandering away from the shelter of the village; through sale by a king or relatives from financial need, or because of the captive's unsavory character, notably criminals or debtors; even through a person selling himself during bad times, such as a drought; and, lastly, through raids specifically aimed at the capture of slaves for market. Sitiki was captured in this last way, as the result of a slave raid on a village.

The reason for the family trek a day's journey from the hometown to a village is uncertain. So young a child was likely unaware of whether the village was the destination or a way station on a longer journey. One speculation might be that Deva was in the process of taking his woven cloth to market in Labe. The identity of the other woman who was with the family is never disclosed, although she was likely Deva's second wife. Muslim men were allowed a maximum of four wives, and the addition of a second wife brought an increase in status to the husband. Deva—judging by the age of his children—had reached the time appropriate for taking another wife. If this conjecture holds, then his young son might have been unaware of the relationship, or, if he did understand, Sitiki's later conversion to Christianity may have rendered polygamy a delicate subject.

Slave raids commonly happened at sunrise or sunset, with surprise being the key. The villagers, hearing shots in the distance and being familiar with such attacks, would have made a quick exit to the safety of the woods, while the urban family, accustomed to living in the safety of a walled town, stayed put in the house.

Upon the capture of Sitiki's family, Jene was first stripped of her jewelry and then led off with the other woman. Women were by tradition favored over men as captives in Africa (Klein 1988:67–69). As slave wives or concubines, they fit snugly into the patriarchal family system and, moreover, could endure hard work—even in the fields—as well or better than male slaves. Nevertheless, as the transatlantic slave trade increased dramatically in the eighteenth century, 60 to 80 percent of individuals shipped across the Atlantic were men. Young adult males just coming into their maximum vigor were preferred.

Older adult men were a problem for the slave traders. They were considered rebellious, likely to flee their captors and, if able to escape, to know where their homes were and how to find their way back. Family men, such as Deva, tried to protect their wives and children and were often killed in the attempt. Sitiki believed that to be his father's fate.

Children were a different story. Being young, escaping and making their way back home was not usually possible. Also, because of their youth, they were trainable and could be taught to fit into the slavery system. From the age of four or five, children were able to learn the easier tasks and, in many African societies, they were thought to have reached adulthood, for purposes of work, by the time that they were eight years old.

Customarily, family members were separated from each other to prevent collusion and escape. Thus, Sitiki found himself carried off by an unfamiliar man on horseback. These captors were probably Muslim horsemen of the Fulbe group.

Maures pillants un village Nègre.

Sketch circa 1780s of "Moors plundering a village for slaves"—note the small child
perched behind his captor as Sitiki reported in his narrative. Albert and Shirley Small
Special Collection, University of Virginia Library. By permission of University
of Virginia Library, Charlottesville, Virginia.

The next day after his capture, Sitiki met his mother walking in a cavalcade
at the crossroads. In a last act of nurturance, she gave him some "groundnuts"
(peanuts). He, in turn, seeing his little brother brought along on horseback,
shared some of the nuts with the little fellow. Sitiki ends this part of the narrative with the gripping sentence, "I never saw either of them again." Many
times, he must have wondered what happened to his mother and brother,
possibly shipped to the Americas as he was.

Slavery in the African System

As an old man writing many years later of his adventures as a newly captured
slave, Sitiki says no more about his family in the narrative and instead details
his sojourn in Africa. Unlike many other slave narratives that tell of the horrors of mistreatment, Sitiki's did not, either because he hadn't experienced

such abuse or, perhaps, because he was narrating this account to his former master. The resilience of his personality begins to emerge here and continues as he relates the events of his life.

The first town—Seko or Sulko—that was reached by the marauders was the seat of the governor's residence. Fixing this town as Segu, the principal town of the pagan Bambara group, is tempting. However, Segu was situated some fifteen hundred miles from the coast. The travel time, distance, and even the terrain description would put that town too far inland.

Lined up with the other captives, Sitiki was not chosen by the governor's constable who picked a few of the captives to remain in the town. Instead, he was again transported on horseback and taken to the home of his captor. He described how he "was unable to hold out any longer" and that all the clothes that he had were "a little sac and no head covering." Under the ministrations of the captor's wife, he was put to bed after a warm bath. Summing up his kind treatment, he said, "I got good treatment wherever it was my fortune to go."

This good treatment was not an isolated instance. The Scotsman, Mungo Park, the first white man to explore this part of West Africa in 1796, said unequivocally that he did not "recollect a single instance of hardheartedness towards me in the women." He remembered finding them unfailingly kind and compassionate (Park 1893 II:72). Park contrasted this with the men whose treatment of him seemed to vary with ethnicity, religion, and other factors.

Sitiki found the house of his captor different from the dwelling where he had lived with his family. Salih Bailali, a West African man enslaved in the same era, described two main forms of dwelling house in that section of Africa. One was of clay, square, flat-roofed, usually with two rooms. These were the houses commonly found in towns and probably the sort of house that Sitiki knew as a young child. The other form was round one-room huts, common in the villages, and constructed of sticks, plastered with clay, and roofed with grass or palm thatch. Inside these rudimentary dwellings, a bench circled the walls (Wilks 1967:147). On such a bench inside such a palm-thatched hut, Sitiki's benefactress put the exhausted young boy to bed.

Afterward, two days were spent in a canoe on a river. Since he believed that they went upstream, they probably headed west toward the coast on the Niger River or one of its tributaries, as the Niger flows northward and eastward with its headwaters in the Futa Jalon mountain range.

Again they came to a town, the seat of a local governor, where Sitiki was bought by that official and then given to another man. Then "my owner," as he calls him, took him to a place a day's journey away, where he remained for a year. This rapid exchange was probably part of the complicated chain existing among the many small political constituencies that covered the landscape in that era.

Placed on a sheep farm for a year, Sitiki was given the job of tending the sheep. In many parts of the world, sheep herding was considered a job for children, and here the practice also served as a kind of slave schooling. Some years earlier, Venture Smith, Guinea-born, was placed in a similar setting. One conclusion was that "the habit of strict obedience to orders, which Venture first acquired during the year he spent on the sheep farm, entrusted with watching the sheep, earned him the high regard of his [new] master" (Starling 1988:78). This one-year internship was likely intended to break very young children into a life of slavery and was an integral part of the complex slave trading networks that existed in eighteenth-century West Africa. According to Pope-Hennessey (1968:195), the capture and routing of children into the slave trade was a much more frequent occurrence by 1750. Such a training ground for young slaves developed, of necessity, in response to increases in slave exports by Europeans.

Slavery within Africa antedated the arrival of Europeans by many centuries, tracing its usage through a long history adapted to local cultures and to social and economic arrangements as well as environmental factors. Although varied in expression, commonalities existed in the internal slavery systems regardless of the locale. African slavery existed traditionally as a domestic institution, as opposed to the economic exploitation that became characteristic of slavery in Europe and the Americas. Generally, tribes in Africa were founded on descent groupings, usually with a patriarch (or sometimes a matriarch) serving as leader, judge, and distributor of favors. While alliances sometimes occurred with other groups for war or other purposes, the domestic units were characteristically self-contained, working ancestral lands, staging wars, engaging in small skirmishes, or worshipping and celebrating together. The kinship group provided identity and security for its members, negating some individual freedom of movement in exchange for protection, secure bonding with others in the lineage, and prestige (Bohannon 1964:105–107).

In the African system, slaves were simply lower-status persons in the extended kinship group. As such, they could rise in stature during their lifetime through a fortunate marriage, demonstrated bravery, good deeds of benefit to the kin group, manumission, or other means. In most parts of Africa, the children of slaves were born free. Consequently, after a few generations, the original slavery was forgotten or unimportant.

By the time of Sitiki's birth in the late eighteenth century, this early indigenous slavery system had eroded considerably as slaves became valuable merchandise in the transatlantic trade. More properly put, slavery still existed in the old kinship mode but, by then, existed side by side with the flow of slaves out of Africa to a different kind of servitude. These systems, rapidly changing in parallel, created chaos in West Africa with internecine warfare erupting with great rapidity. Yesterday's alliance could quickly shift into today's war.

The Coffle

At the end of the year herding sheep, Sitiki experienced the common fate of being marched to the coast in a coffle for eventual sale. Descriptions of these coffles vary. A coffle consisted of a long line of slaves and their "slatees" (the guards accompanying them to the coast). The term "slattee," used by Mungo Park, is derived from old English, meaning one who thrashes or punishes others. This designation aptly describes the rigors of the forced march to the coast. Other individuals were sometimes added, traveling along with the coffle for safety in hostile territory. Commonly, the procession was single file because of the frequent narrow passages and to avoid escape into the bush.

The slaves were secured to each other in various ways. The captives, according to the description of Mungo Park who traveled with a coffle as the guest of the leader, "are commonly secured by putting the right leg of one and the left leg of another into the same pair of fetters." Then batches of four were secured around the necks with "twisted thongs." Guards were stationed between each four-person group. Each slave sported a bundle secured to the

Sketch of "Slave Coffle, Central Africa, 1861." Albert and Shirley Small Special
Collection, University of Virginia Library. By permission of University of Virginia
Library, Charlottesville, Virginia.

head, increasing the burden of the march. At night, precautions against escape included additional fetters put on their hands and "sometimes a light
chain passed around their necks" (Park 1893 II:135). Depictions of children
in coffles show them tied or chained to adults, sometimes between two adults
and not next to other children.

Progress was slow and tortuous on the narrow and constricted paths, often taking a month or six weeks to reach the coast from the interior of Africa.
Sitiki said that no river was crossed. These treks to the coast with captured
Africans were confined to the dry season when some of the river beds were
dry. Likewise, G. E. Brooks (1998:153–155) indicates that 1630 to 1860 was a
drought period in West Africa.

Sitiki's account of his experience in a coffle seems unique in some ways.
Coffle stories by adults stress the hardships: the fatigue, starvation, cruelty,
and sense of hopelessness and despair. Sitiki's tale, in contrast, shows a sense
of wonder and adventure at each new happening or exciting thing along the
way. Although unpleasant parts may have been deleted from the story, his

original exuberance shines through his words. All of his senses were engaged. The people, the terrain, and most of all the animals captured his imagination. He saw an ostrich and was initially frightened. He also said that he saw buffalo, elephants, camels, goats, and deer, and heard a lion's cry but did not spot the creature. He tried buffalo and elephant meat and found the latter "tough and unsavory."

The people were also remarked on: "a half dozen men with guns" accompanied the coffle. This description compared with those of other coffles indicates that the number of slaves was small, probably fifty at most. The guards accompanying the coffle are described in a side notation in one version of the narrative as being "men marked according to their nation," providing some speculation that the guards were not Muslim but rather from an indigenous religious group that used scarification or tattoos as tribal or lineage identification.

Sitiki showed interest in the "priest" who was along, the "rosary" that he carried, and the fact that he ate and slept separate from the coffle. This religious man was probably a Marabout, an itinerant Muslim teacher or holy man. In the strictest sense, "Marabout" is defined as "a Saint or a venerated descendent of a Saint," who is considered to "exercise a spiritual influence, grace, or blessing" (Glasse 1989:258). In West Africa, they served an economic or political function as well as a religious one.

Sitiki's reference to him as a "priest" is understandable as he was familiar with Catholic priests in St. Augustine. When he first came to Florida in Spanish times, it was a theocracy and remained largely Catholic for many years after the U.S. Territorial period began. The "rosary" carried by the African holy man was probably the string of prayer beads favored by Muslims. The coffle must have been traveling during Ramadan when fasting is required, as this man only ate and drank before day and after sunset.

We must pause here again to consider the animated description of this overland journey. The seventy years between the experience and the recounting distilled in Jack's mind the marvels of the trip to the exclusion of the discomforts. Add to this the fact that children are naturally resilient and, unless seriously deprived, retain their sense of wonder under appalling circumstances. As a child, Sitiki was allowed more freedom than the adult men. His description of running away from the ostrich indicates that he was allowed to go unfettered at least some of the time. Samuel Gamble, a slave ship captain of the time, noted that at night "The Women, Boys & Girls, are loose, but a good guard over them" (Mouser 2002:100). According to his description, Sitiki was shackled to a man part of the time, probably when the coffle was on the move, but he does not speak of this as a hardship, although it must have been. In noting the lack of negative comments in Sitiki's description of the coffle he traveled in, it is well to remember that he was recounting his story to his former owner, a white man. As to the route of the trip and the final destination on the coast, conjecture is necessary. Since the trip to the coast was by several means—horse, canoe, and on foot—and included the year on the sheep farm, the distance from Sitiki's home to the coast could have been anywhere from two hundred to four hundred miles. Putting together the trade routes at the time and clues in the narrative, the Rio Pongo region on the coast is postulated as the end point of the journey. This guess fits with the sequence of terrain described: a rocky plain or savannah, then a forested area adjacent to the Futa Jalon mountain range, the mountains themselves, and finally the coastal plain with its dense tropical vegetation.

Rio Pongo is thus thought by this author to be the destination of the coffle, although no certainty is possible. Another possibility might be Moria farther south. The Rio Nunez, another British settlement north of the Rio Pongo, is also a possibility. Life in these various British coastal factory settlements which processed slaves for export was nearly the same in each locale. The description in the next section is of the Rio Pongo. The picture of the life that Sitiki led there gives us a general idea of the experience of a servant slave around 1800 to 1807 anywhere on the West African coast.

House Slave in a British Settlement

The coffle taking Sitiki to the Atlantic coast with other slaves might have ended at any of three major British port settlements for the slave export trade: the Rio Nunez, the Rio Pongo, or the Moria area. The outlet at the Rio Nunez was known for its good harbor, permitting deep-draft vessels that were much preferred during peaceful times. The Rio Pongo—with its protected and winding watercourses and questionable harbor—was of great advantage as the 1793 war between England and France began and later as the slave trade was declared illegal by several nations (Mouser 2002:x). Moria to the south was the third possibility among British slave settlements on the West Africa coast.

While the Rio Pongo is described as the most likely possibility, its characteristics, nevertheless, are somewhat similar to the other two ports. Upward of twenty trading stations existed in the Rio Pongo region from 1790 to 1808. One source mentions that two dozen Europeans were living on the banks of the main river and its tributaries in 1800 (Mouser 1971:326).

As the coffle neared the end of its journey before coming to the sea—presumably near the Kissing settlement—Sitiki saw the strangest creature yet, a white man. He reported looking "at him closely to see what kind of being I could make out." He made no other observation, whereas other Africans might remark on the pink-white skin, the red ears, and the general ugliness.

Possibly, this white man had come from one of the slave factories to purchase prime slaves. Customarily, the imminent arrival of a coffle was heralded by the exchange of gunshots used as messages, thus allowing factory owners or their representatives to intercept the entourage in advance of the final destination (Conneau 1976:76). This particular trader turned down the purchase of the boy because of the stipulation that he was to be sold as a package deal with the "old man."

Nevertheless, Sitiki's wait for a new master was short. The coffle came to a river, perhaps the Rio Bangalan, a tributary of the Rio Pongo. Eight or nine miles from the sea, strong tides left the banks of the river bare for a mile or more at low tide. They arrived at a slave factory or trading establishment owned by a man named Taylor who purchased Sitiki. To date, Taylor has not been definitively identified. As one possibility, a captain named Taylor sailed the ship *Tartar* to the "Rio Pongus" on June 18, 1806 (Donnan 1935:517). For a man to own a slave factory in Africa and also own or captain a ship in service of the slave trade was not uncommon.

At Taylor's establishment, Sitiki saw a ballroom and was amazed when he

Photograph of the ruins of a British slave factory, Rio Pongo, West Africa.
Photographer Daniel L. Schafer. By permission of Daniel L. Schafer, Jacksonville, Florida.

found "gardens, beasts & poultry with everything for convenience and comfort." He beheld for the first time a "store of goods." He was kept shackled
to the old man for three weeks, after which he became a house servant in the
establishment and may have helped in the store.

In the ballroom, Sitiki might have observed diverse activities. A large
room of this kind served as a general meeting room, but was frequently used
for dances as the designation suggests. Dancing was always a favorite activity
in West African society, enjoyed whenever Africans got together and often
a form of religious expression. Whites participated as well in this convivial
pastime on the African coast. Among other matters, celebrating with dancing and singing was a way of cementing economic alliances among native
participants, traders, and ship captains.   The European and African cultures blended in a strange amalgam in these coastal trading stations. According to Joseph Hawkins, an American who shipped aboard a slave vessel
as an officer to manage the financial part of the enterprise, some unsavory
activities took place. When he landed at the Rio Nunez in the late eighteenth
century, Hawkins observed that the factory owners lived in some luxury and
often entertained the ship captains and other visitors in a lavish manner:
". . . the morning beverage of Madeira or Lisbon wines, spirituous liquors, or
the more palatable *liqueurs* of the *belle nation*, circulate during the forenoon,
which is devoted to visiting from house to house" (Hawkins 1797:155). After
imbibing all day, dinner was spread at the most prominent establishment:

> . . . the board is scarcely spread, and the guest seated when the *debauch*
> begins; for their behavior is unrestrained by that taste for decorum
> which is always inspired by the society of amiable and accomplished
> women . . . . They come to the table nearly intoxicated, and before din-
> ner is completed, they become downright drunk . . . . The coarse jocu-
> larity of destroying their apparel or wasting the food is their amusement
> . . . . The meats are even occasionally dashed about the heads of the
> best humoured, or most patient of the company, and the empty dishes,
> plates, and tables are demolished to show the spirit of the party, and the
> lengths to which they could carry a *joke*. (Hawkins 1797:155–157)

The black wives were then charged with taking the drunken men to their
respective quarters.

There is a note of caution here. J. D. Fage has questioned Joseph Hawkins's account describing his 1795 trip to West Africa, especially whether he actually traveled inland to gather slaves for export. Some questions also arose as to which coastal ports he visited. Since he was ill and published his story once back in America, he may have exaggerated his adventures in order to profit from the book. The above dramatic account contains perhaps a kernel of truth but is probably embroidered to intrigue readers (Fage 1991, 18:83–91). Regardless of what Sitiki may have witnessed of such events, these incongruities afforded the young boy an opportunity to live in a way station between two worlds, instead of being unceremoniously shunted from one continent to another, the common fate of most victims of the African slave trade.

Since the Rio Pongo was a well-known trading complex at the time, several descriptions exist of the delta area where Sitiki found himself. When Joseph Hawkins claimed that he was there, he gave a euphoric account, which could have been exaggeration for effect. When landing at the "Reyo-Pongo" on February 5, 1797, Hawkins reported seeing "a Handsome harbour within the northern bank, three leagues from the mouth of the river, close to the shore, in view of a luxuriant country, low, and thinly covered with scattered woods and picturesque collections of reed. The opposite side of the river appearing in perspective, more bold and rising in proportion to its distance . . . the banks were however covered with the most exuberant richness, the air was not intensely hot, the clearness of the sky charming, and the nights delightfully serene and tranquil." He found that "the number of beautiful islands formed by the windings and divisions of the river into branches" afforded the abundant fish "a secure and peaceful retreat" (Hawkins 1797:14–15). Certainly the slaves procured and brought there must have found it far from such a peaceful retreat.

The Rio Pongo delta—as was the case with other trading communities on the coast—had a distinct culture. The customary pattern for the English, as well as other nationalities on the Guinea coast, was for a prospective trader who wished to start a factory to first establish a relationship with the chief of the principal native group in the locality. Cumba Bali and his subchiefs ruled the Susu, who held sway in a narrow strip of the coast verging on the Rio Pongo complex at that time. This location could have been a bit of good fortune for Sitiki, as Susu is one of the Mande languages, and

Taylor's African wife was probably a Susu who could communicate with the young slave.

As part of a new trader's relationship with an African group, a daughter of one of the local dignitaries usually became the new entrepreneur's wife. Commonly, the offered wife was the daughter of a slave wife or a concubine. The advantage to both sides of the bargain is obvious. The chief held some control through his daughter and the children born of the marriage. In this arrangement, the native wife served as a linkage with other Africans in business negotiations and, all things being equal, she was in a better local position than she would have been if she had stayed within her family of origin. The white trader, for his part, acquired a great advantage by being embedded in the local network through his African wife. The family was the main institution in Africa, and anyone outside of the extended lineage complex was considered an enemy or at least suspect.

Marriage between a European man and a native African woman was solemnized in the African tradition. As described by Conneau, whose friend Edward Joseph was married to an African woman in a three-day ceremony in the Rio Pongo, such a union was far from a Christian rite and often considered a loose connection by a white man. In this case, the honeymoon was a short one. Joseph, needing to leave Africa, seems to have abandoned his bride with no backward look, necessitating a sad return to her people (Conneau 1976:107–116).

When such a marriage did last, the arrangement put the African wife in a brokerage position between the two cultures. The wives, as well as their mulatto children, were sometimes sent to England to be Anglicized and Christianized—to learn the ways of the English and, in the case of the females, to learn the cooking and cleaning that was thought proper for the domicile of her white husband. At that time, Liverpool was the main training ground for those sent to England from West Africa as that city had eclipsed London and Bristol as the prime mercantile city in the later years of the slave trade. There, visiting Africans found an enclave of blacks and mulattoes like themselves.

Some of these trading families on the African coast became quite extensive, developing their own special blend of African and European culture. Sitiki heard of a man named Fraser (misspelled in the narrative as Frasier) while he was still in Africa. The original John Fraser was an American with a trading station in the Rio Pongo region and a New World base in Spanish Florida, as well as contacts in Georgia and South Carolina. He drowned in the St. Johns River near his Florida home in 1813. As was often the case, Fraser conducted the transatlantic aspects of the family business, usually leaving the African factory on the Rio Bangalan to the management of his mulatto son, also named John. The younger John had four African wives and numerous children, one of whom, Elizabeth Fraser Skelton, born in 1800, later became one of the most prominent female entrepreneurs on the Guinea coast.

The other man of whom Sitiki heard in Africa and later knew in Florida was Zephaniah Kingsley. Kingsley was descended from a prominent family in England. He operated a large establishment in northeast Florida and was engaged in slave trade on the West African coast. He made alliances with several African women, one of whom, Anna Madgigine Jai Kingsley, was well-known and even managed Laurel Grove, one of Kingsley's plantations in Florida. In Africa, Kingsley's main center of operations was in Senegal to the north, while Fraser's factory was in the Rio Pongo region (Schafer 2004).

As is the nature of groups in isolated locations, one person commonly rises to prominence and power over his fellows. In the Rio Pongo, John Ormond assumed that eminence. The Ormond factory was near the Fraser trading station close to the Rio Bangalan. By 1827, some twenty years after Sitiki left, things had changed. When the slaver Theophilus Conneau became the clerk for John Ormond II, the mulatto son of the first John Ormond from the Rio Pongo—this worthy referred to as "Mongo," meaning leader—was in possession of a sizeable harem of wives given to him by native leaders as a means of currying favor and providing linkage with the interior (Conneau 1976:71–74). John Ormond's power, nonetheless, was fading because of his dissolute lifestyle and poor management practices.

Taylor, Sitiki's master, may have been a newcomer in the neighborhood as only one wife is mentioned. The time periods are unclear here. How long Sitiki lived and worked in this factory, while not mentioned in the narrative, may have been as long as five years, or even more, before his master died. He reported holding Taylor's head as he died, but whether this scene implies a close master/slave relationship or, more likely, happenstance, remains conjectural. The young house slave was privileged to attend his master's funeral and was surprised to see a dozen white men at the ceremony, whom he thought were English.

White traders on the African coast, such as Taylor, frequently suffered early death. Tropical diseases were ubiquitous, and Europeans lacked immunity. Mosquito-borne diseases took their toll, especially in the rainy season. Dengue or "African fever" caused flu-like symptoms coupled with severe headaches and joint aches. Rarely fatal, it weakened the victim for months. Theophilus Conneau, during an extended stay in the Rio Pongo region as a clerk for Mongo Ormond, contracted the disease and suffered from delirium. Afterward, the "continued fever" left him feeble, an "emaciated, poor ambulating living skeleton whose stomach could never be satiated and whose limbs underwent for a long period a diurnal concussion of two hours' duration, caused by the fever and ague" (Conneau 1976:86–88). The "breakbone fever," as it was also called, was clearly debilitating. Malaria, however, along with excess consumption of alcohol, frequently dispatched a white man in his first year or two of residence in Africa. If he did endure the first period of seasoning in the tropical coastal climate, he had a good chance of remaining to make a fortune. Often, men were forced to take the risk because of exile from England due to family circumstances or their own legal entanglements. As Captain Gamble observed during his stay on this tropical coast in 1793–1794, "a European richly deserves what he gains here" (Mouser 2002:52).

After the proprietor's death, Taylor's African wife went to England, and Sitiki was shifted to "another like establishment." Whether bought by another man or simply rented out while Taylor's wife stayed in England is a point in question. Nor do we know how long he stayed in the new location. The owner of this second factory remains unnamed in the narrative. As to the location, we have a clue. Sitiki mentioned that "the native people who live about the settlement are called Juluf." The Juluf were probably the Jolof, a subgroup of the Wolof. The Wolof, who were Muslim, lived just below Senegal and the Rio Gambia. Some were herders, moving stock from season to season; others were sailors, engaging with merchants in port commerce. If this reference matches, the second factory's location was farther north from Sitiki's first location on the coast.

In any case, Sitiki was in a position to see the operation of a slave trading business in several locations. The typical factory had the living quarters for the proprietor and his family upstairs in the main building, while the store, warehouse, and barracoon were downstairs and outside. The word "barra-con," properly spelled "barracoon," is only mentioned once in the narrative and that in a subheading, possibly as an editorial addition by Buckingham Smith. In its usual configuration, the barracoon consisted of a holding area for the slaves: a yard or section of the factory used for incarcerating the captives who were awaiting sale and shipment overseas.

The barracoon, certainly one of the horrors of the slave trade, was similar to a cattle pen. Unroofed, it had a long sheltered area running down the middle where the men were shackled in the shade. The women and children, less likely to escape, enjoyed the freedom of the enclosure but were nearly always under the surveillance of one or more guards, often with loaded and pointed guns. The number of slave deaths in the sultry, insect-infested environment of the holding pen occurred in proportion to the length of incarceration. The outdoor courtyard next to the holding pen led to the dock on the river. Many of these factories were little forts of their own, guarded by canon. Fortunately, as a house slave, Sitiki would have observed, but not experienced, the cruelties of the barracoon.

The West African trading culture at the turn of the century was a strange mixture of white men, African women, their mulatto progeny, native village leaders from nearby, the constantly appearing coffles from the interior, and the slavers who came to port to buy and ship their human cargo and other goods. Caution was always needed to prevent riots among the captured Africans or to keep slave rustlers—either black or white—from stealing slaves, the most valuable "commodity" in the eighteenth-century West Africa coastal trade.

White men living in these trading stations exercised little control over the hinterland, as the interior lands remained totally African for centuries. In fact, instances occurred in which a factory owner (or owners) ran afoul of the nearby king who controlled the trading network. In these cases, the African group simply moved away when matters became onerous, leaving the Europeans without business (DeCorse 1998:222–223).

Sitiki's interlude on the African coast as a slave under the British system occurred at a unique time in the history of the African slave trade: the beginning of the end of legal slave trading on the West African coast. The last half of the eighteenth century was an era of strong antislavery sentiment in England, culminating in the passage of the Abolition of the Slave Trade Act by Parliament in March 1807, which prevented engagement in the African slave trade by British traders. Not content to just suspend their own slave trading operations, the British traders likewise intended to prevent other nations from engaging in this lucrative transatlantic traffic. Their motive was economic, if vengeful. Subsequently, British naval ships were dispatched to anchor off the coast of Africa to intercept slave ships heading for the Americas and to search factories on the coast for slave trade activity. The recaptured Africans then had the chance of being repatriated, but often to an unfamiliar locale, much to their disadvantage.

The Church of England, an institution on record for many years as against enslavement, took another approach. Along with the British abolition of the slave trade came a thrust to colonize the coast and educate the local populace, particularly in the ways of Christianity and its "ideal" moral values. England was then undertaking the brand of mission colonization already adopted in other parts of the world, while, ironically, maintaining plantation slave systems in the Caribbean that were some of the most brutal operations in the Americas. However, this missionizing in coastal settlements began after Sitiki left Africa.

But, before leaving the African period of Sitiki's life, we should note the elements that conspired to single him out for special treatment. He did not get pushed into the mass of plantation-directed Africans sent to the Americas. What special traits can account for his purchase as a house slave and, therefore, the fortunate delay in his shipment overseas? The clear light of intelligence perhaps, good looks, personable demeanor, and good health must all have counted in his favor. Much to his advantage, he learned some English by exposure to the British factory owners and traders while still in Africa, so he arrived in the United States in a more advantageous position than most of his fellow Africans. His adjustment in the formative years of his life to an often turbulent environment showed an adaptive and accommodating nature that was to serve him well in his future life.

III

THE MIDDLE PASSAGE
TO CHARLESTON

6

"Like a Son"

Eventually, Sitiki was sold to the captain of an American brig, a slave ship headed for the south Atlantic coast of the United States. From shipping information, we can determine that the brig appears to have been the *Sally*, owned by Graves of Charleston and captained by a man named Brown (Donnan 1935:524).

The brig *Sally*, a square-rigged ship of medium tonnage, was one of the coastwise vessels pressed into service during and after attempts to stop the slave trade, replacing the slow and cumbersome "snow" vessels of earlier times. The "slaver," as it was called, carried a great deal of sail and its hull was built for speed (Chapelle 1965:130–174). These ships had an advantage over the cumbersome snows weighing one thousand to two thousand tons, which were used by the British during the eighteenth century and earlier. The British and Americans largely abandoned the use of the snows, as well as other large vessels, as they were far from swift and difficult to maneuver.

The year that Sitiki experienced what was called the "Middle Passage" was 1807, as the shipping company's log noted that the brig entered the port of Charleston that year. The term "Middle Passage" was an old-time seafarer's expression relating to ocean currents along the transatlantic passage. At the time of the slave trade, the term was used in reference to the middle

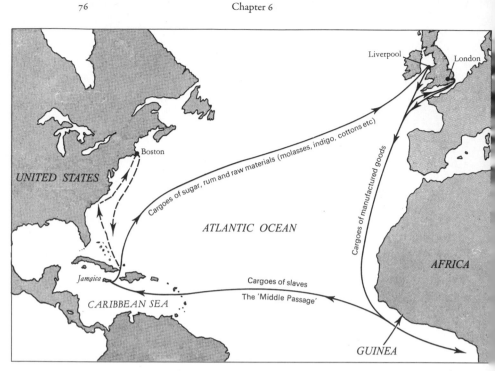

Adapted from eighteenth-century map of triangular
slave trade across the North Atlantic Ocean.

of three crossings (from Africa to the Americas) in a triangular route taken
by slave ships. The other two crossings were the initial trip from Europe to
Africa and the return trip from America to Europe (Palmer 1995:32–37).
The brig's crossing, if the noted year is correct, occurred just before the
passage of the British Anti-Slavery Act of 1807. After that, British ships
patrolled the African coast to apprehend slavers of all nations, impound the
ships, and set the slaves free.

Sitiki could have boarded the ship at the embayment at the mouth of the
Rio Pongo or farther to the north. What were the emotions of this African
boy as the forest-cloaked shore of Africa punctuated by small tributaries
receded from view, giving him a last glimpse of his homeland? Or was he
perhaps asleep, as slave ships often departed at night to avoid the anguish
of the slaves who were certain that their fate would be terrible. Rumors
regularly circulated that the white captors were cannibals.

This part of Sitiki's narrative is related in a flat but positive way, which tells us nothing of his emotions except the pleasure of having the freedom of the ship. Sitiki—then somewhere between the age of twelve and fourteen—was fortunate to be a cabin boy, a more favored position than that of a common slave. Doubtlessly, his ready wit and ability to speak English were in his favor. Sitiki's experience aboard the *Sally* was atypical, since Captain Brown bought him not as part of the cargo, but as a personal slave, companion, and servant. We do know that he was berthed with the captain and allowed to do as he pleased.

Today, the idea that Sitiki berthed with the captain and slept in the bed with him is puzzling. Yet privacy is a modern notion. Until about 1830, people lived in closer association with one another and sleeping alone was avoided, if at all possible. Old diaries even speak of looking up a stranger to share the bed in order to avoid being lonely. So Captain Brown and his "son" slept together in the captain's berth and doubtlessly scratched the same fleas—ubiquitous as those insects were on shipboard—and listened to the scrambling rats.

He does not speak of himself as a cabin boy, but perhaps he did not know the term. Writing from a distance of many years, he concluded that he was treated "like a son." Cabin boys were usually white, but African cabin boys were not unprecedented. For example, Antonio, a bright and lively nine-year-old mulatto, was the cabin boy when the well-known slave mutiny took place aboard the schooner *Amistad* in 1839.

Sitiki had plenty of opportunity to play with the other children aboard. On most slave ships, the children and women were brought up on deck more often than the men. In the early years of the nineteenth century, an average of 10 to 14 percent of slave cargo was children, so Sitiki had plenty of playmates. As to the games played, "Panyaring [kidnapping] was so common that, during the Middle Passage, children used to play at kidnapping one another" (Mannix 1976:91). Children's games, of course, characteristically mimic the dramatic events of their own times. The serious and deadly game played upon them and their families by the slave traders was transformed into play, thereby decreasing their anxiety and fear.

While he probably associated with the children on the ship, Sitiki speaks dispassionately of the "blacks" as though he were not one of them. He may have watched the men and women dancing on deck as required to maintain fitness. He was privileged to dine on better food than the other slaves were allowed. The cargo slaves on this particular vessel were given "all of the cowpeas and rice that they could eat" and were furnished with a pint of water each day. His report of the water allowed was a scanty ration that could have led to hyperthermia. The slave runner Conneau, in describing treatment of the slaves during the Middle Passage, reported that water was "given three times a day, a half pint each time" (Conneau 1976:89). Neither of these amounts was enough to quench thirst or sustain the body adequately. The food ration aboard the *Sally* indicates that this shipload of slaves was better treated than slaves on other ships where food was meager or strictly rationed. The fare was a standard one, although Captain Brown may have had trouble provisioning rice, which was in short supply in the Rio Pongo region at the time because of the accelerating trade in that decade. Cowpeas, a warm climate crop (of which black-eyed peas are a modern variant), were then much used as forage for animals as well as common fare for enslaved or poor people.

In the best-run ships, the slaves were fed breakfast at 10:00 a.m. and then allowed up on deck, weather permitting, until the evening meal at 4:00 p.m. They usually took their meals ten at a time from a common vessel. After the evening meal, they were secured below decks in cramped and unsanitary conditions, the horrors of this practice being well documented. The best slave ships, those especially built for the trade, were ventilated with portholes, but the need to close these in stormy weather made life insufferable for the slaves so confined.

Only two slave deaths were reported for this crossing, an unusually small number considering that the average death rate at that time ranged from 14 to 20 percent of slave cargo. Even if the ship carried fewer than one hundred slaves, the record is good with a probable mortality rate of 2% or less. The largest number of deaths aboard slave ships was from the bloody flux (dysentery). Other diseases also took their toll: malaria, measles, smallpox, scurvy, yellow fever, both bubonic and pneumonic plague, and last the dreadful "guinea worm," ubiquitous in tropical Africa even today. *Dracunculiasis*, the scientific name, translates as "afflicted with little dragons." These worms found new hosts among the tightly packed slaves below slave ship decks. Whether a ship avoided a decimating outbreak was a roll of the dice. Another subtler element was the emotional one. Untold numbers of slaves suffered so much anguish and despair that mental depression and sometimes death ensued. At the very least, acute depression contributed to immunosuppression and increased the slaves' vulnerability to physical illness.

A little known fact is that the crews, especially those of the poorly oper-ated ships, had a higher death rate than the slaves. The members of the crew were usually the dregs of the waterfront, picked up for low wages or even pressed into service against their will. Because of the need to control and service the slave cargo, twice as many crew members were needed aboard a slave ship than were required on an ordinary merchant ship. At the end of the voyage, the crew, unlike the slaves, would not bring a profit. In fact, the crew members would have to be paid, and so, in certain respects, were often given poorer treatment than the slaves. The doctors on some slave ships even refused to attend to the crew because their contracts called for slave care only.

By the end of the eighteenth century, a doctor or surgeon was employed aboard most slave ships, a practice required by law in some countries. Sitiki mentions that one doctor was on board his ship. The doctor would make twice daily rounds to inspect or attend the ill. If he spotted a slave on a hun-ger strike, a common way to attempt suicide, a gruesome instrument known as a "mouth opener" was employed.

Arrival and Stay in Charleston

The brig *Sally* apparently made a smooth crossing, as nothing in the narrative suggests otherwise, arriving in Charleston some time in 1807. Sitiki's first glimpse of the east coast of North America disclosed to him a low-lying and scrub-covered coast interrupted by frequent waterways. While this terrain was not totally unlike that of his former home, the familiar rocky headlands and mountain ranges of Africa were missing.

Charleston lies on a low, sandy peninsula behind a splendid harbor formed by the Ashley and Cooper Rivers. Because of the town's advanta-geous setting, numerous ships were typically in the harbor and many of these were slave ships. Toward the end of legal slave importation, Charles-

ton was the primary entry port for the slave trade in the United States, su-
perseding Virginia, which had been eminent in the trade in earlier times.

Unpleasant in those days was the raw sewage floating in the bay, a result
of the huge volume of water traffic. Even worse were the dead bodies floating
about. Several documents tell of this horror. On April 21, 1807, an inquest
was held on the body of "a negro woman floating near the Market dock,
known to be a recently arrived slave because of her blue flannel dress." Common practice among unprincipled ship captains was to throw overboard the
bodies of those slaves who died before sale in order to avoid burial expenses.
The jury in the market dock case brought in a verdict of "death by the visita-
tion of God." The coroner offered a reward of one hundred dollars to those
exposing the perpetrators of so "inhuman and brutal a custom." The coroner
also added the information that three more corpses were drifting in the bay,
causing an "effluvia very prejudicial to the health of the passengers" on boats
plying in and out of the busy harbor (Donnan 1935:527).

Those "passengers" like Sitiki, arriving on slavers, might have seen such
sights, but the stench of even the best-kept slave ship was so bad that the "effluvia" in Charleston harbor would be hardly noticeable. Some arriving slave
ships could be detected by smell as far away as ten miles down the river, if the
wind was right.

For various reasons, the slave trade in South Carolina was banned from
1786 to 1803, although slavers continued to unload their cargoes illegally
during that period. There was good reason in 1803 to reinstitute the African slave trade. Cotton was becoming the preferred crop. Slaves born in the
United States, who were accustomed to growing rice and indigo, were un-
acquainted with how to plant, weed, and harvest cotton, whereas recently
imported slaves from some areas of West Africa—including Sitiki's likely
birthplace—were familiar with cotton culture.

The brief five-year interlude from 1803 to 1808 when slaving was legal brought an enormous trade in slaves to the vicinity. Charles Lambert
(quoted in Donnan 1935:521) gives the figure of 15,626 slaves imported into
Charleston in 1807, the last year of legal importation. Charleston was indeed
a boomtown when Sitiki arrived as one of that number.

Nevertheless, Sitiki was not offered for sale in Charleston but instead continued for a time as Captain Brown's personal slave. He and the captain first

stayed at a hotel run by "a one-armed man." The location of this hotel could not be determined, although it was most likely in the old section of town. The captain left Sitiki at the hotel while he went about tending to business, doubtless the task of selling the slave cargo. Left to his own devices, the high-spirited youth indulged in boisterous activity, annoying the guests and staff. In his own words, they "had to go from there, as I was noisy at play and the captain was obliged to be much about."

Sitiki and Captain Brown then removed to the boarding house of a "Mrs. Ellis." The Ellis family was well-known in the Charleston area, with most of the family members owning and living on plantations outside of town. However, the 1810 census for Charleston in Christ Church Parish listed two Ellis women, Ann and Mary, living in different locations (U.S. Census 1790–1880). At the time, Ann was living at 35 Church Street in a building built in 1770, which is still standing (U.S. Census, Charleston County 1810). The structure is now known as the Young-Johnson House. We have a strong clue that this location may have been the boarding house mentioned in the narrative. In the 1809 Charleston Directory, a "Daniel Brown, ship captain," is listed as staying in the boarding house at 35 Church Street (Hrabowski 1809:8). That the Daniel Brown listed in the Charleston Directory was the captain of the brig *Sally* is a reasonable though not definitive assumption.

IV

IN THE FAMILY
OF JOSIAH SMITH

Savannah, Then North to Connecticut

Early in 1808, Captain Brown sailed from Charleston to Savannah with Sitiki aboard along with "two slaves for sale." The two brought to Savannah for sale did not include Sitiki, who evidently assumed that he would remain as the captain's slave.

The brig landed in Savannah on February 9, 1808. As the narrative described, "here finding that we should have to go to sea again Captain Brown reluctantly concluded to part with me and in so doing it was his care that I should not get into a cotton plantation or a rice field." The decision to "part with" Sitiki—although the young boy may not have been aware—was probably a result of the enactment of the Slave Importation Act that went into effect January 1, 1808. The new law would make carrying any slaves aboard his ship problematic for Captain Brown. The language of the law was specific:

> Be it enacted . . . that from and after the first day of January, one thousand eight hundred and eight, it shall not be lawful to import or bring into the United States or the territories thereof from any foreign kingdom, place or country, any Negro, mulatto, or person of colour, with latent intent to hold, sell or dispose of said Negro, mulatto, or person of colour, as a slave, or to be held to service or labour (U.S. Statutes 1807 II:426, #445).

Therefore, Captain Brown sold Sitiki in March 1808 to Josiah Smith, a merchant of the town. According to Sitiki's description, Smith was an imposing man, about thirty-five years old and "in the vigor of life." Smith had been in the town for about six years when he bought the boy. His "Store and Counting Room," located on Burroughs and Sturgis Wharf, was a well-respected and solid establishment. The merchandise for sale was diverse: "pipes of country gin," rum, brandy, coffee, loaf sugar, wheat flour, and beef led the list of business transactions. Other items for sale were blankets, whips, great coats, and even "velvet pantaloons for gentlemen" (WSA 1756–1957, 846 box 18, folder 464; box 8, folder 77). From time to time, Josiah Smith offered special lots of just-arrived merchandise, such as "10,000 lbs. prime St. Domingo Coffee" (CMSA VII:5, March 17, 1807). The item most often mentioned was brandy, a favorite of the time and in demand to exchange for slaves on the African coast. He probably stocked other merchandise to use in the African trade as was then common with port city merchants.

In addition, Josiah Smith operated as an agent. He solicited clients in a series of newspaper advertisements: "Josiah Smith offers his services to Planters and others in the Factorage and Commission Business and hope from strict attention to merit their patronage" (CMSA, XII:17, November 3, 1807). He was an agent for the ships *Kesiah* and *Luna* among others. Smith also took an active part in the community. He was a "fireminder" for the Derby Ward, where his shop was located, and an active member of the Chamber of Commerce (CMSA, XII:47, August 1, 1807; July 24, 1807, p. 2, col. 1).

Josiah and his wife Hannah were first cousins, originally from Watertown, Connecticut. At the time that Sitiki was purchased, the rest of the family consisted of Josiah, a two-year-old named after his father, and a female infant. Since Savannah was booming as a port town during the first decade of the nineteenth century, just as Charleston was, Josiah Smith must have decided to make his fortune in this southern city. The first documentation of his presence in Savannah is in 1802. He evidently still maintained his northern ties, as he belonged to the New England Society of Georgia and was elected "Counselor" of that organization in 1807 (CMSA, XII, May 5, 1807).

With the kind of operation in which he was involved, Josiah Smith had other slaves when Jack was purchased in 1808. An item of particular interest appeared in a local newspaper on May 15, 1807, about two runaways:

Two African Fellows, About 25 years of age absented themselves on Sunday last—One is a stout yellowish fellow, and his country name Aneumanah; the other very black, considerably marked with smallpox but is otherwise scarified in the face and answers to the name of *joxoi*, neither of them speaks any English. A reward of *five dollars* for each will be given on their being lodged in the Goal of this city. [signed] Josiah Smith. (CMSA XII:22:3, 1807)

No record was found as to whether these two Africans were recaptured. Jack's value as a multilingual slave (West African languages as well as English) was an asset to himself and certainly to his master.

When Smith came aboard the brig, Sitiki noted that "he liked and bought me." In their first exchange, he asked the boy his name and, on being told, renamed him "Jaques" on the spot. From then on, this African with a Muslim name considered his name to be Jack Smith. This action of his new master may seem harsh, as in the Americas, name changing has often been cited as indication of the debasing action taken by white slave holders. However, in the African tradition, an individual often assumed or was given a new name when his or her status changed. In other instances, the names used were situational (Abrahams and Szwed 1983:100–104). In our own culture, a woman has traditionally assumed her husband's last name upon marriage as a new status. No matter how this name change is regarded, the boy's Americanization had officially begun.

Another slave, a thirteen-year-old girl, was bought about a month later. Together, the two slaves stayed with the Smith family for many years. At this point in the narrative, Buckingham Smith recorded a section on the back of a page about this female slave. The name given is not the same in later censuses, but the handwriting is unclear in the narrative. The best guess is that her new American name was Judie or Indie, while her African name was Poli. As children, she and her brother, Bayo, were captured near their town of Mayon in West Africa when they were out in the woods gathering wild berries. A few years later, they were shipped to Charleston. The boy was sold there and the girl was sold in Savannah to Josiah Smith. Buckingham Smith obviously interviewed her at the time Jack's narrative was written, as he wrote down five vocabulary words that she remembered. Jack and Judie, as they were henceforth called, were barely out of childhood when they met. Since they were in constant day-to-day association for many years, each offered the other some continuity and stability.

The time Jack spent in Savannah afforded him a brief chance to renew his work skills in a mercantile establishment, this time in an American setting that was both a slave plantation and an importing economy. However, Jack's stay in Savannah lasted for only three months before he moved with the Smith family to Watertown, Connecticut.

North to Connecticut with the Smiths

The two and one-half years that Jack spent with the Smith family in Connecticut are sparsely documented in the narrative, yet what we are told is illuminating. The journey itself impressed Jack. The family and the two slaves went north by sea to New York and hence took a packet (a regularly scheduled small boat) to New Haven. From there, they traveled by horse-drawn stage to Watertown, apparently Jack's first trip by such a conveyance.

Watertown, located some thirty miles inland from New Haven, is on a small tributary of the Naugatuck River. More important at that time, Watertown was on the old New Haven to Albany route, one day's journey from the coast and thus a convenient overnight stop. A little more than a decade before the Smith trip, the road was upgraded and named the Straits Turnpike.

The reasons for the Smith's move back to the family farm in Connecticut are obscure. Possibly both push-and-pull factors were operating. On the one hand, the 1808 embargo on slave importation into the United States caused a realignment of the economy, particularly in the Atlantic coastal cities dependent on the trade. Although illicit slave trade continued, merchant establishments, such as Smith's in Savannah, were wholly or partly dependent on legitimate slave trade and suffered economically after the enactment of the 1808 law.

On the other hand, the economy in Connecticut was also changing. Before 1800, family farms in Connecticut were characteristically self-sufficient. However, the soil was wearing out, and many families consequently moved west. In any case, the thin soil and rocky terrain were better suited for raising stock than crops. In inland Connecticut, sheep raising was the most successful, although the native stock then common on family farms was of inferior quality. Between 1800 and 1815, rams and ewes were imported from Spain to improve the stock; the merino breed was advantageous with its high-yield and high-quality wool. The interest in this new endeavor was so strong that some referred to the enthusiasm as "merino fever." Better quality wool increased exports. The turnpikes, built to serve the interior farms in that same era, aided the new economy. Likewise, southern markets for wool and mutton were opening up, as extensive plantation development was then taking place in the southern states. This new trade was funneled through the ports of Charleston and Savannah (Bidwell 1916:300–340). Josiah Smith was in an advantageous position to work both ends of this economic chain with exportation from his farming enterprise in Watertown and with his contacts in Savannah.

A tempting speculation is that Jack's knowledge of sheep herding was part of his value in Connecticut. He certainly speaks of the occupation as "the old one," emphasizing his own experience. Just as American agriculturalists were finding that West African slaves familiar with cotton cultivation were of great value in the South, those with experience in pastoral locations commanded respect for their expertise in New England. Thus, the move to Connecticut helped Jack to begin maximizing things for himself with the Smith family, as he was already familiar with the care of "hair sheep." On the Watertown farm, Jack was also responsible for care of the other stock: cows, chickens, and a horse.

The original Smith farm may have been larger, but forty acres certainly belonged to the family by then. Later, after Josiah's death in 1825, Hannah sold the Watertown property to Abigal Seymour (SJC CCR 1833, box 354, folder 70).

Two houses were located on the property. One belonged to Hannah's widowed mother, who, because of the cousin relationship, was Josiah's aunt as well as his mother-in-law. At the time of his marriage to Hannah, Josiah built the other house. For two months in 1808, the family stayed in the main house with the mother/aunt. Their own dwelling may have needed repair or perhaps was occupied when they arrived.

Neither house was a mansion. In the early part of the nineteenth century, the houses of even well-off farmers were far from sumptuous. Many of these houses were no more than two or three rooms, heated by an open fire and lit by candles at night. The advent of room stoves and the use of oil lamps were at least thirty years in the future.

For Jack and Judie, the new location was their first experience of cold weather. Unlike Georgia, where they could spend their nights in an unheated kitchen or other outbuildings, the arrangements in the New England winters would certainly be different. In any case, for Judie, who cared for the children, sleeping near her charges was part of her daily routine as a female house slave.

The family most likely attended Episcopal (Church of England) services at Christ Church, a relatively new structure built a few years earlier on the foundation of an old church. The Congregational Church was across the street on the town common and next to the turnpike. The juxtaposition of these churches was part of the religious history of Connecticut. During the Revolutionary War, Tories continued as members of the Church of England and soon found themselves outcasts. As a result, the state of Connecticut became a Congregational Church theocracy of sorts, leading many counter-revolutionary families to locate elsewhere, which may have been one reason why the Smiths moved to Georgia in the early 1800s. A few years later when the family returned to Watertown, the situation had settled down. Nevertheless, Josiah Smith had an eye for opportunity throughout his life, which may have brought about that move as well as the other moves in his life.

Jack and Judie were rarities in Connecticut in the early nineteenth century. While the number of slaves remained at a relatively high level until 1790, gradual abolition began to decrease the numbers. By 1810, only 310 slaves remained in the entire state of Connecticut among a population of 262,000 persons. Conversely, 6,453 free "coloured" persons were listed in the census.

Slavery in New England, even at its zenith, was never the plantation type of the South. The usual pattern was for a few slaves, often only one or two, to work on a farm along with the white family and perhaps one indentured person or more (Pierson 1988). By long tradition, a slave in New England, although legally chattel, informally occupied a role between bondage and indentured servitude. To meet the needs of the diversified economy, a slave in New England needed to be versatile and certainly more skilled than the

Sketch of Watertown, Connecticut, circa 1836, showing two churches: Episcopal and Congregational. The Connecticut Historical Society. By permission of The Connecticut Historical Society, Hartford, Connecticut.

average slave on a southern plantation. With some exceptions, slaves were thus more respected and treated more kindly in New England than in other states on the Atlantic seaboard of the United States (Greene 1969:101,327). The American slavery system was never uniform, but distinct regional variations existed, as Jack was beginning to discover.

Jack recalled "little of interest" that occurred during his sojourn in the North. Yet he began learning to read, an endeavor that eventually flowered into the effective literacy useful to him later when he became a Methodist minister. The mother of his mistress, he tells us, taught him the alphabet and began his instruction in spelling. Why he did not go any further than "baker" is a mystery. Perhaps the death of the infant daughter of the family brought Jack's education to an abrupt halt.

He may have become aware of the sadness of the family in a symbolic way, as he recounted an incident involving a dead bird. He prefaced the account with the comment that it "has influenced to the full extent my after life." It began innocently enough. In a surge of adolescent spirit, he threw a stone at a bluebird and killed it. He carried the dead bird to his mistress's mother as a prize. To his consternation, she moaned, spoke words of sadness, and shed some tears over the little carcass. His reaction to this incident was so strong that he never tried to kill or capture a bird again. His restraint seems remarkable, since a strong market for mockingbirds and cardinals existed in St. Augustine when he first arrived there. These birds were taught Spanish songs and sold in Havana.

The well of deep feelings expressed in retelling this incident might possibly have an echo from his early life. At the time of his capture in Africa, he was too young to attend the Muslim school. As mentioned, a preschool boy was commonly taught at home in West Africa by a grandmother or other older woman in the family. Thus, Jack may have been sensitive to upsetting the grandmother of the Smith family household. On her part, the elder woman must have been emotionally upset at the time over the death of her infant grandchild, and thus overreacted to the death of the bird.

8

Back South and Captured Again

Jack's statement that "the vicissitudes and movement of the family everyway concerned my own fortunes" illuminates the involuntary nature of his condition and effectively foretells the next chapter of his life. Rivaling his adventures in Africa, his narrative for this eight-year period reflected the frontier ferment and chaos in south Georgia and north Florida.

Josiah Smith, for his part, took advantage of every situation to enhance his own economic and social position, and what better place to do this than on a frontier. In 1810, he moved his family and slaves from Connecticut to St. Marys, Georgia. The United States had by then been in existence for a little over two decades, and the borders of the former colonies were expanding to the west, north, and south with Florida thought to be the next frontier. With Smith's prior knowledge of Georgia and his mercantile, shipping, and farming interests, he was in a strong position to take advantage of the situation. He set up in three places. He first located the family on a farm outside the town of St. Marys. Then he established a summer house at the northeast part of Cumberland Island across the bay from the town. In this island location, the family enjoyed the cool summer breezes while Josiah monitored the ocean traffic nearby.

Within two years, Josiah obtained land from the Spanish government on Amelia Island at Fernandina in Florida. The towns of St. Marys and Fernandina are separated from each other by the St. Marys River, the conventional boundary between Georgia and Florida, and a permeable boundary in the first decades of the nineteenth century. As described by Jack, the Smith place in Fernandina was near the residence of "old Fernandez," next to the Fernandez corn and cotton fields and behind the wharf of Fernandina New Town. The Fernandez house was still standing fifty-four years later when Jack dictated his narrative.

For a time after the move to St. Marys, the slave Judie was still in Connecticut, left there to take care of the baby of another family, the Smith infant having died. No record exists of when Judie rejoined the family, but she was probably back by the time that Thomas Buckingham Smith was born on October 31, 1910, on Cumberland Island. Jack Smith was about fifteen- or sixteen-years-old at the time and had no way of knowing that this child, always known as Buckingham rather than Thomas, would eventually be a significant part of his life.

Often, the narrative is elusive as to the family members' whereabouts during these times. We do know that part of the family was in Fernandina in 1815 when another child was born, a girl named Anita. Josiah Smith, meanwhile, was taking advantage of the embargo on importation into Spanish Florida during the War of 1812 by shipping much-needed food and other necessities to St. Augustine, certainly a clandestine activity. Later, he used this activity as leverage to acquire more land in Florida. On May 15, 1815, he petitioned for and received one thousand acres on a "strip of pineland running [from] the banks of St. Marys River to Bell's River." He expressed the wish to raise cattle on the rural property, knowing that the garrison in St. Augustine was chronically short of beef. He also reminded the governor that he "rendered service . . . not only to the town but to the whole province of Florida, during the revolution of 1812, risking his person and property [by mean of] securing the remittance of a brig loaded with provisions, that put an end to lack of food in the town" (WPA, SLG, 1941, 5:93–94).

The three locations occupied by the Smith family provided a good base to carry on Josiah's commercial operations. Likewise, his master's far-flung interests and absences brought Jack into a position of greater responsibility. At times, he was in charge of the house at St. Marys during Josiah's absence.

If Jack was responsible, he was also vulnerable. Admiral Sir George Cockburn, after leading the British to sack the capitol in Washington, D.C., in the War of 1812, headed south in 1815. The Admiral's intention was to persuade slaves to run away from their masters, thereby, he hoped, ruining the plantation economy of southern Georgia (Mahon 1972:349–370). Altogether, fifteen hundred men were deployed by the British in Georgia.

Between January 9 and March 18, 1815, Admiral Cockburn landed and took possession of St. Marys and Cumberland Island. The north end of the island, where the Smiths lived for part of the year, was a mixed area of whites and slaves who worked small farm plots, some using vacant land, others working on shares or land of unclear ownership. At that time, an estimated 225 slaves were present on Cumberland Island.

By chance or design, when Admiral Cockburn and his men captured slaves, Jack was not on Cumberland Island but at the farm on the Georgia mainland where, in Josiah's absence at Fernandina, he had been left in charge. Jack tells of his capture this way: "The British, then at war with us, having come there [the farm near St. Marys], the officers carried away the furniture and took me to their quarters." They had positioned themselves at the south end of the Cumberland Island at the estate of Dungeoness. From there, they set about making forays onto the mainland to persuade other slaves to leave their masters.

The slaves captured by Admiral Cockburn were given a chance for freedom and could either go to Nova Scotia with the British or enlist in the British Navy (Bullard 1983:4–85). As Jack tells the story, "My master applied for me from the admiral, who gave consent that I should go, if I chose, and Cockburn gave me a written license to pass where I might like."

Josiah Smith, having left Jack in charge at St. Marys, had been apprised of the situation. When he made his request to the admiral to release Jack, he used his connection with the Spanish to provide substance to his request, saying that he had already applied for Spanish citizenship. In the meantime, Sebastian Kindelan, governor of Spanish East Florida, formally protested the capture of slaves of Spanish masters by Cockburn and firmly requested that this Spanish chattel property be returned to them.

As it developed, Jack stayed as a slave in the Smith family. The factors leading to Jack's staying cannot be fully known and could have ranged from a decision based on options available, to convenience or even preference, or on a kind of loyalty to his master. As it turned out, the seven hundred slaves who did sail for Nova Scotia with the Admiral's fleet did not fare very well on the whole. In fact, a rumor circulated that Cockburn sold some of the freed slaves back into slavery.

When Jack and some others were released, he returned to the Smith family home. How much pressure was put on Jack to remain in slavery, either by his owner Josiah Smith or by the Spanish authorities, remains a question not answered by Jack in narrating this event to Buckingham Smith fifty years later.

Eventually, the Smiths found problems in Fernandina to be intolerable. During those early years of the conflict, what was called the "Patriot War"— a spinoff of the War of 1812—had expanded into Florida. Alternatively referred to by the Spanish as a rebellion, the war was an attempt by Anglo frontiersmen to add Florida to the United States with the covert support of authorities in Georgia (Cusick 2003).

To add to the turmoil in north Florida, ambitious adventurers saw Fernandina with its good harbor as up for grabs. Informally, it became a freetown. As early as 1809, the bay at Fernandina was crowded with ships bringing in supplies and food for the Spanish and exporting cotton and rice, principally to England. Slave ships also used the harbor, with some of the human cargo being smuggled illegally into the United States. Opportunists such as Josiah Smith used the chance to reap huge profits through the transfer of goods, although no record exists of any slave trafficking on Josiah's part. This free-for-all in Fernandina was a constant irritant for the Spanish authorities in St. Augustine to the south.

Fernandina continued in turbulence. Movements for republican government were rampant in Europe and the Americas saw the beginning of attempts at independence that, in the subsequent century, flowered into extensive decolonization. Outsiders seeking power and fortune saw the general imbalance as a wide-open opportunity to take over Florida by way of Fernandina, precipitating skirmishes with the Spanish trying to hold the province and the frontiersmen bent on making East Florida a part of the United

States. The Scottish freebooter, Sir Gregor McGregor, captured Fernandina late in 1816 and set up his own government. Others followed suit.

Staying in north Florida was no longer safe or wise for the Smith family. Because of the uncertainties, if not outright dangers, in the Amelia Island area, the Smiths returned to St. Marys, Georgia, where they remained until 1817. We do not hear in the narrative about Jack's activities during that two-year stay. Since other slaves had been acquired by then, he likely became the head slave with increased duties. In 1817, Josiah Smith made the far-reaching decision to move to St. Augustine, where the family continued to live for many years. Jack spent many more years as a slave of the Smith family but ended his years in St. Augustine as a freedman.

9

Working with the Smith Estate

Jack was with the Smith family during volatile times in St. Augustine under three regimes: the end of the Second Spanish Colonial period (1817–1821), the U.S. Territorial period (1821–1845), and finally Florida statehood (1845–1882). Minus the three years that Jack was with Buckingham Smith in New York during the Civil War, he remained in St. Augustine for sixty-five years.

Early Years

The Smith's entry into St. Augustine was hardly auspicious, yet it provides a glimpse of the trust placed in Jack. In early May of 1817, the family boarded a schooner loaded with their effects and headed for St. Augustine. At the harbor—always a difficult one to navigate—they encountered a west wind that prevailed for a week, making entry impossible. Finally, Josiah Smith gave up and returned north, where the family then took the land passage to St. Augustine. Meanwhile, Jack was left in charge of the schooner still loaded with the furniture and, after a few days, sailed south again and at last entered the harbor on May 17, 1817. There, he saw "the city behind an island fourteen miles in length on the north end of which at the entrance to the bay is a white sand reef, covered with numberless sea birds." With that view, Jack's life in St. Augustine began.

Upon the Smith family's arrival in St. Augustine, Josiah Smith lost no time in establishing himself. Immediately, he acquired a land grant to the west outside the walled town. The plot was 9.4 acres, a long and irregular piece of land stretching from the street at the edge of town (now Cordova Street) then west, ending on the shores of the San Sebastian River. To the north was *tierra del Gobierno* (government land), where the Old Powder House was located, and to the south was land owned by Jose Sanchez, a free person of color.

Josiah's application for the grant named the Smith family and their slaves: "Don Josiah Smith, Dona Ana Smith, Josiah sixteen years, Buckingham eight years, Hannah four years; Male Slaves—Jack twenty-one years, Boston twenty-five years, Hartford twenty-six years, Augustin twenty years, Ceasar eighteen years, Pompey twenty-one years, John twenty years, Harry twenty-eight years, Katto sixteen years, Marcus seventeen years; Female Slaves—Judy nineteen years, Fanny twenty-one years, and Cloe seventeen years" (WPA, SLG, Vol. V, 1817: 99–102). Jack is the first slave on the list. Other documents procured by the Smiths also list Jack first, even though other slaves were older than Jack. This placement may indicate his leadership role. Another explanation is that the name order reflects accession by the family.

The Smiths were among the first suburban settlers in the west of town, breaking new ground in some respects, although garden plots had been tended there previously. Josiah Smith built a two-story house in the middle of the land. No photograph was found of this house, but on an early map the house appears sizable and is graced with a tower. Eventually, several outbuildings were constructed, including slave cabins. The cabin built especially for Jack is described as near the main house, likely in the vicinity of present day Carrera Street. Jack lived for many years in that location, farming the land and cultivating the orange grove.

Josiah Smith was always ready to undertake several ventures simultaneously. In his customary fashion, he opened a mercantile establishment in the town. Its exact location is unknown, although most such stores were located on the Street of Merchants (now Charlotte Street) close to the waterfront. Here, he sold whatever the townspeople needed, even importing some items in his own boats. After the deprivations of the Patriot War, the needs of the town and its hinterlands were many. From Jack's narrative, we learn that the

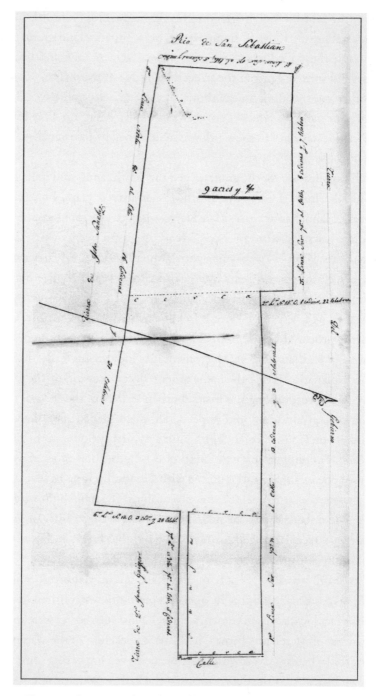

Plat map of property of Josiah Smith's heirs on the Rio de San Sebastian, nine acres, May 16, 1817. Florida State Archives, Tallahassee.

Photograph circa 1869 of Jack Smith in front of his cabin. Photographer E. A. Meyer. Photographic Collection, St. Augustine Historical Society. By permission of St. Augustine Historical Society, St. Augustine, Florida.

store was stocked with, among other things, wax, wagons, and iron pots. The latter was such a scarce commodity that those imported for sale in the Smith's store were often stolen before they ever reached the store's shelves. Iron pots were valued for many uses, such as cooking one-dish stews and soups, laundering, and processing various materials.

From documentary and archaeological evidence, we know that any store of goods also stocked foodstuffs and ceramic ware. Availability concerns aside, tastes in food in largely Hispanic St. Augustine would have varied

Photograph of a portrait of Hannah Smith, 1819, mother of Buckingham
Smith and longest owner of the slave Jack Smith. Photographic Collection,
St. Augustine Historical Society. By permission of St. Augustine Historical
Society, St. Augustine, Florida.

some from those of Anglo Savannah. Citizens of St. Augustine desired not
only British-made ceramics—the creamware and slipware popular at the
time—but also, from long tradition, the Spanish ceramics such as majolica
and other wares imported from Havana. Earthenware, as always, was sold as
well. Some wares were locally produced and others were imported (Cusick
1993:159–165). In the last photograph (a stereopticon) of Jack seated before
his cabin, some earthenware vessels are on a ledge in the background. Jack
was familiar with such vessels from his days in Africa.

Jack evidently served in several capacities in the store, including as clerk,
which was especially needed as Josiah was frequently elsewhere. By that time,
Jack was experienced in business, being already familiar with a store of goods

in Africa and having clerked in Josiah Smith's store in Savannah. The St. Augustine store's location gave Jack a unique window for observing the town and waterfront, which was certainly put to advantage when he later undertook description of the town.

The Smith Family Changes

The year of 1823, two years after Florida became a territory, seems to have been a crucial time in the Smith family. Buckingham's older brother, Josiah, died during that year, making Buckingham the oldest child in the family. That same year, Buckingham, then thirteen years old, and his sister Anita were confirmed in Trinity Episcopal Church. This chain of events might have led to Jack Smith's conversion to Methodism, also in 1823–1824.

To complicate matters further, Josiah Smith embarked on yet another venture: He went to Mexico as part of the U.S. legation. This plan was arranged as early as 1819 when West Florida became part of the United States and the annexation of East Florida was impending. One assumes that Josiah was fluent in Spanish by that time, having dealt extensively with the Spanish population in St. Augustine. Thus, to the U.S. government, he probably seemed a logical choice for the position. Entrepreneurial as always, Josiah Smith took the opportunity in Mexico to invest heavily in silver and tin mines. In 1824, Buckingham went to Mexico City to join his father and, therefore, was with him when Josiah died suddenly in 1825. Dealing with this calamity was surely a maturing experience for a lad of fifteen.

According to Josiah Smith's will, Buckingham became a ward of his uncle, Robert Smith, of New Bedford, Massachusetts. In Massachusetts, Buckingham attended Trinity College in 1826. Then, upon graduation, he entered Harvard Law School. After obtaining his law degree, Buckingham joined the law office of Judge W. P. Fessenden in Portland, Maine. Soon, Buckingham became a Justice of the Peace there. He did not return to Florida until 1839, at which time he established a law practice that continued for eleven years and sporadically for more.

What happened to the Smith family in the fifteen years that Buckingham was gone? Obviously Hannah Smith, Josiah's wife, was in charge of the family's commercial interests in Florida after her husband's death. She was an able manager and dealt with myriad problems with a sure hand. With Jack's help, she may have kept the store open, although whether this was the case has not been verified. She certainly dealt with the landholdings and other business matters. The plantation lands near Fernandina were in dispute. The surveyor George Clarke, in some ways an unprincipled person, had questioned part of the claim while Josiah was still alive. Hannah now had to deal with this messy situation. In 1828, she also confirmed the title to another plantation of 488 acres on the Palatka Trail west of St. Augustine. In the watershed area of the St. Johns River, this prime agricultural land was well watered by Deep Creek on its southern boundary and Cypress Pond on the northeast corner. The land was located near the present day town of Hastings. In proving the claim, she had to explain the absence of activity on the land. James Hall was called as a witness, being familiar with that location. He considered settlement there impossible because of "Indian Difficulties . . . the murders that were committed throughout the country," and because the area was overrun with "negro thieves" (WPA, SLG, Con S 64; DG V 386, 397).

Hannah also tracked down the individuals who owed money to the estate. For example, an Episcopal minister, Ambrose Hull, who owned a large plantation at New Smyrna, owed Josiah's estate a sum of money that Hannah was unable to collect. Undaunted, she was instrumental in forcing the property into bankruptcy so that she and others could collect on Hull's defaulted loans. When Buckingham returned to St. Augustine in 1839 and set up a law practice, his mother, not surprisingly, was one of his best clients. In the early years of her widowhood, Hannah also managed the farmland with the help of thirteen slaves who were all in their prime working years. Jack was the ranking slave. He was in a position to help with the Smith's St. Augustine enterprises and, presumably, to supervise the work of the field slaves.

In the meantime, Buckingham found time to pursue other activities. For a time, he was secretary to the territorial governor, Robert Raymond Reid. He also served as a member of the St. Augustine City Council. More exciting activities included night patrol duty in 1840 during the Indian scare near the end of the Second Seminole War. The following year, he became a member of the Florida Territorial Legislature. In 1843, he married Julia Gardner of Concord, New Hampshire, and purchased twenty-two acres, later known as the Garnett Orange Grove, where he lived with his new wife. The location was

Photograph of the home that Buckingham Smith built in 1845 in St. Augustine.
Photographic Collection, St. Augustine Historical Society. By permission
of St. Augustine Historical Society, St. Augustine, Florida.

well north of his mother's land. Buckingham built a two-story house with
many windows and multiple porches, a structure well-suited to the warm,
moist climate of St. Augustine.

The airiness of the building proved to be a liability, however. Much to the
chagrin of the family, a slaughterhouse was built immediately to the west,
giving off a horrible stench when the west wind blew in the summer. Equally
bothersome were the flies—attracted by the raw meat—that necessitated
covering all of the windows with muslin. Buckingham addressed the issue
with the city council, pleading with the members several times to see that the
nuisance was removed from their vicinity, all to no avail initially, although
the processing plant was ultimately shut down (COSA, CCM 1849).

Nevertheless, in spite of this unpleasantness, Buckingham set about planting an orange grove using some experimental techniques that he wanted to
try with Jack's help. Culturing oranges was a lifelong interest of Buckingham's. In fact, a description of ways to preserve oranges for shipping was
a section within his first attempt at writing, which became Buckingham's

second career. Although he does not receive credit, his innovative idea was
to wrap each orange individually in a piece of paper, a practice that later became common and persists to this day. Many of the drafts of Jack's narrative
are written on sheets of thin blue paper, possibly left over from this orange-
packing operation.

After the young married couple moved into their new home, Jack presumably stayed on Hannah's property, although he may have worked in the
orange groves on both plots of land. When paying his taxes a few years later,
Buckingham listed two slaves and a carriage as valuable items. Neither of
these slaves was Jack, as he was one of the thirteen slaves listed for Hannah
Smith on the same tax list. Hannah also owned a horse. Of the 324 house-
holders on the town's tax list in 1855, only nine households contained ten or
more slaves (COSA, TL 1855). The Smith's affluence was evident from their
ownership of numerous slaves and extensive land.

Jack's failure to mention either Hannah Smith or Julia Smith in his narrative is an interesting omission, considering that he was under the supervision
of one or the other from time to time, and especially as Hannah was his legal
owner for more than three decades. This omission may possibly have more
to do with the form that Buckingham wanted the narrative to take than any
reason on Jack's part.

Foreign Affairs Brought Home

The year 1850 brought more changes. That year Anita Smith Porter, Buckingham's sister, died. She was married to an army officer and, thus, had been
absent from the family home for some years. Also, on September 9, 1850,
Buckingham was appointed to serve as secretary to the U.S. legation in Mex-
ico, his father's old position. He and his wife stayed in Mexico for two years.
Rather than investing in the mining of precious metals as Josiah had done,
Buckingham spent his spare time mining the archives in Mexico City for
materials on Spain's occupation and dealings in Florida and the southeast
Spanish Borderlands. The Smiths were poorly paid and housed in Mexico.
They "lived in genuine privation, the income of the representatives of the
United States being so small that the diplomat would go out on mule back
into the provinces hunting rare volumes" (*St. Augustine Record* 1941:1,8). By

then, Buckingham was already launched on a self-appointed writing career with two publications to his credit, engaging as well in active correspondence with scholars throughout the country.

Meanwhile, Jack Smith was busy in his quiet way, carving out a significant place for himself in the town in addition to his agricultural work on the Smith's lands. After joining the Methodist church at the age of thirty, he became one of the key black members of the congregation. In 1845, his efforts to raise money enabled the building of a small church on donated land. He preached there from that time, although he was not officially sanctioned as a preacher until after the Civil War. Jack's life as a preacher in St. Augustine is covered more fully in Chapter 11.

From 1852 to 1855, Buckingham and Julia Smith were again in St. Augustine. During that time, Buckingham undertook a vigorous campaign to be appointed to the U.S. legation in Madrid. In this effort, he made many trips to Washington. In desperation, he wrote to Peter Force, one of his scholarly friends, "See if anything can be done to get me to Spain or Cuba—I am tired of talking and have no force except with book men." He was so obnoxious in this endeavor that a friend wrote to E. G. Squier, "Smith is still hanging on here [Washington, D.C.] . . . thinking that perhaps some time or other somebody will send him to Spain, if only to get rid of his importunities. Perhaps so, but in the meantime it is necessary to prevent him from spoiling his chances—supposing him to have any—by keeping him out of mischief . . . so pray lend him a hand to set him to work" (Wall 1941:15). E. G. Squier, a historian working on South American materials, and Buckingham were good friends. Their letters to each other were in a "jocular" vein, in contrast with the staid and proper letters that Buckingham exchanged with other scholars.

In spite of this dim view of receiving the desired appointment, Buckingham was finally successful. He and Julia sailed to Spain in 1856, where he occupied the position of secretary to the U.S. legation for five years. During that time, he described himself as "on the crest of the wave" in his vigorous pursuit of acquiring manuscripts in various Spanish archives. He was well received in Spain, having what was described as a Spanish "tone" in speech and action, which he absorbed in his years spent in Spanish St. Augustine. Consequently, he was furnished with a royal order of the widest extent, allowing him to work in various cities in Spain and visit their archives. Several significant private family archives were opened to him as well.

Halfway through Buckingham's service in Spain, Julia returned to St. Augustine to take care of family business because of Hannah Smith's declining health. On behalf of Buckingham, Julia sold the twenty-two acre orange grove to Fones McCarty in 1857. She then moved their own household to the old Smith property where Hannah and her slaves, including Jack, still lived.

The next year, Hannah Smith died at the age of eighty-three-years old. Buckingham came home to settle the estate and, as part of the probate of the will, transferred ownership of the twelve family slaves to himself for three thousand dollars. The sale took place at the family home on May 2, 1859. The place of the auction indicates a foregone conclusion that Buckingham was to be the buyer. The slaves were named, probably in order of age or status, as "Jack, Mary, Judy, Katy, Tena, Nancy, Sue, Lucy, Jane, and Ellen" (SJC, CCP, Box 165, Folder 9, 1859). They were "sold in one lot being mostly of 2 families." Three or four were "aged Negroes." Katy was characterized as "insane" and separately assessed at fifty dollars. Sue (or Susan) had two or three small children, which presumably brought the total up to twelve or, if Katy was included, thirteen. The number of slaves in the household was about the same as the number owned by the Smiths for many years. The only difference was the gender imbalance, since Jack was the only adult male, whereas many males were listed in earlier censuses.

Buckingham and Julia then returned to Spain, presumably leaving Jack as unofficial caretaker with the agreement of several of Smith's friends to assist, if needed. After several years, tragedy struck again when Julia Smith fell ill. The couple was returning to St. Augustine from Spain so that she could be under her mother's care, but she died on shipboard the day after Christmas in 1861.

Buckingham's return to the United States had another overriding element. He and the ambassador of the United States to Spain, Augustus L. Dodge, were at odds almost from the beginning of their association. The ambassador asked that Buckingham be removed from the legation near the time of Julia's illness. Buckingham fought this dismissal tenaciously. The two men were very different. Whereas Buckingham was a polished gentleman, Dodge was a provincial person from Iowa; Buckingham regarded the position of diplomat as a gentleman's occupation, whereas Dodge was a career bureaucrat despite his inadequate knowledge of protocol; Buckingham was a fluent Spanish speaker, whereas the ambassador's linguistic ability was limited. Buckingham ridiculed the ambassador to the authorities in Washington, while Dodge charged that Buckingham was insubordinate and prone to go off on his own to visit Spanish archives. Both charged the other with being arrogant. From the record, one guesses that both versions held some truth. Dodge tried to get Smith into a physical conflict (Buckingham hinted at a duel challenge in his letters to the authorities in Washington), a suggestion that was beneath the dignity of a gentleman like Buckingham who considered his challenger to be of lesser stature. In a last effort to convince President James Buchanan (1857–1861) and Secretary of State Lewis Cass that Buckingham should be recalled, Augustus Dodge charged that Buckingham Smith was supporting a woman and child in Madrid. While probably untrue, the acrimonious altercation between the two men had reached such a level that Buckingham was dismissed. In disgust, he returned to St. Augustine, but at the same time proudly carried with him a harvest of documents gathered in Madrid and other cities in Spain. These documents, most of them painstakingly copied from the originals, formed the basis for Spanish Borderlands research for many years and are still used today.

For the rest of Buckingham's life, he and Jack were in close association, managing the orange grove together and collaborating on the introduction of new plants. Buckingham must have spent much of his time writing books based on his research, as his major works were published within the next few years. Still, restless as ever and chronically short of cash, he undertook a new venture for a short time—buying and selling books and also publishing books and reports—but found the trade not to his liking and likewise unprofitable.

The Civil War

A short time later, the Civil War was imminent. Although a slaveholder, Buckingham was an avid Unionist. As with many others in the North during antebellum times, he believed that the war was about keeping the nation together, not about slavery. To his consternation, he was informed in 1862 that the Confederate States of America in Florida was in the process of confiscating all of the Smith property, probably including the slaves. Florida had the distinction of being among the first few states to secede from the Union. Consequently, the Confederate authorities in Tallahassee went after those not loyal to the South.

Considerably alarmed, Buckingham took several steps. First, he informed the authorities in Washington that northern Florida, particularly St. Augustine, was a Confederate stronghold. Although the matter is uncertain, Buckingham wrote a letter that may have had a minor role in the subsequent occupation of Jacksonville and St. Augustine by Union forces. Union strategists were already aware of the advantage to be obtained by capturing and occupying the state. Consequently, gunboats were dispatched with orders to occupy Fernandina, Jacksonville, and St. Augustine.

Buckingham's second step was to take Jack with him on a hasty trip to New York. There they remained for three years and one week, according to Jack, until the war was over. Jack's absence from St. Augustine during this time leaves a gap in his narrative.

Buckingham and Jack missed some tumultuous times in the town. The Confederate troops were by then deployed west of St. Augustine by the St. Johns River. When two hulking Union gunboats arrived off the coast of the town on March 11, 1862, many families fled. Some of the hardy Confederate women brave enough to stay approached the flagpole on the plaza, axes in hand, and chopped it down so that the stars and stripes flag would never be raised over the town. The scene was a strange one when the Union troops came ashore. At the wharf in front of the plaza, a small group gathered to meet the soldiers—a few Union sympathizers, some old men, and a handful of black men. If Jack Smith had been in town, he, as a ranking person of color, would likely have greeted the officers as they stepped off the boat. Instead, "Daddy Smart," the minister of a small independent Protestant congregation, did the honors. He is supposed to have said, "Gentlemen, I welcome you to our [city], not so much on my own account as for the good of my race" (Cochran 1896:95).

Subsequently, the town was fully occupied with soldiers, their loud band music, and their colorful uniforms, causing a stir in the placid and almost deserted town. The Fourth New Hampshire Volunteers, who generally acted wilder than the regular soldiers, sported the colorful Zouave uniforms to distinguish themselves. One little girl who went down to a store on the plaza to make a purchase was so frightened by the invading spectacle and noise that she ran home and refused to leave her house for several days (Cochran 1896:103–104; Graham 1986:26–27).

If we are to believe the reports of several eyewitnesses, St. Augustine slaves were told that they were free, even before Lincoln's Emancipation Proclamation. General David Hunter, the regional commander, had earlier proclaimed the emancipation of slaves in Georgia, Florida, and South Carolina, which were zones under his command and partially occupied by Union forces, especially in the coastal areas. Consequently, the slaves remaining in St. Augustine in March 1862 were called to a meeting at the Presbyterian Church on St. George Street, where General Rufus Saxton, the local commander, read a declaration of freedom to them with his officers in attendance. Curiously, a Methodist clergyman (name unknown, but described as a "missionary to the contrabands") also attended that meeting. The designation "contraband" in this context referred to property (slaves) confiscated by the Army from Confederate slave owners. As a result of the meeting, a number of the newly freed slaves in St. Augustine left in the next few weeks to join the Union forces or to seek fortunes elsewhere (Anonymous 1862; Cochran 1896:100–115).

Thus, St. Augustine was one of the first places where slaves were apprised of their freedom early in the course of the Civil War. President Lincoln, concerned about this preemptive freeing of the slaves, nullified the Hunter proclamation of emancipation on May 19, 1862, just two months later, but with little effect on those in St. Augustine who by then considered themselves freedmen. Less than a year later, on January 1, 1863, Lincoln issued the official Emancipation Proclamation. The second announcement in St. Augustine—a sort of anticlimax—took place on a vacant lot near St. George Street south of the plaza.

Jack was one of a number of St. Augustine slaves not privileged to hear either one of these freedom speeches. Since his master was a Unionist, Jack had gone north with Buckingham. Other newly freed slaves whose masters left to aid the Confederate cause, such as Emanuel Osborne, Isaac Pepino, and Tony Welters (an accomplished musician), were likewise absent. One of these Confederates was Aleck, the slave of General Edmund Kirby-Smith, who accompanied his master as a servant during the hostilities. Upon being freed after the war, he rose to prominence as Jack did. Aleck, later known as Alexander Hanson Darnes, attended Howard University and became the first black medical doctor in Florida, just as Jack Smith became the first black Methodist minister in St. Augustine.

Jack and Buckingham's stay in New York is the largest blank space in Jack's narrative. Nevertheless, events there may have been more exciting than in St. Augustine. Indeed, Jack counted ". . . the three years and a week I was out of town during the civil war . . . the better part of my life." New York was a bulwark of the Union and had outlawed slavery in 1827. Thus, Jack was in an awkward position in regard to his status while there. Buckingham might have avoided explanation if he simply referred to Jack as a servant. However, New York was not without its own prejudices, having experienced a long period of racial troubles, unlike most other northern states. In 1863, riots broke out in the city after the Conscription Act was passed. Irishmen, who were usually poor and unable to pay the three hundred dollars required for an exemption, resented being drafted into fighting a war to free "Negroes" who would then, they thought, inundate the city and take their jobs. Nor did the Irish like the idea of serving alongside blacks in the army. Before the "Draft Riots" were over, buildings were burned, stores looted, and blacks clubbed and lynched. Even the houses of wealthy whites, who were thought to have initiated the drafting of black soldiers, were sacked and burned (Bergman 1969: 235; Meier and Rudwick 1970:144).

Buckingham returned to St. Augustine briefly in 1864, presumably to check on his property and the other slaves, perhaps leaving Jack by himself in New York. Trusting Jack was by then a given, for master and slave had been associated together with interlocking interests for many years. After all, Buckingham was now fifty-four and Jack around sixty-nine and they had been together for more than half a century.

Concern over the war and his inability to look after his property, including the other slaves, must have taken its toll on Buckingham's appearance. In anticipating Buckingham's trip to St. Augustine, Dr. Anderson felt that warning his mother not to worry was necessary because of Buckingham's wild appearance and manner. On the same trip, Buckingham attended the National Republican Convention in Baltimore on June 7, 1864, as a Florida delegate.

A puzzle exists over whether Jack ever came south with Buckingham during the Civil War. The 1864 Union census, undertaken in 1863, included Jack among people in St. Augustine. Perhaps he accompanied Buckingham on one or two trips and was thus listed as being in town. Another possibility is that Buckingham did not wish to leave Jack behind in New York because of the race riots there (U.S. DOA, SC 1864; McGuire 1991:67–68).

Always in a position to take advantage of circumstances, Buckingham used the stay in New York to write and publish. His book detailing the confusing explorations of Giovanni da Verrazanno was published in 1864. Another work, *Narratives of Hernando de Soto*, written during the New York years but published after the Civil War, is generally considered to be Buckingham Smith's most significant book (Smith 1866).

The Orange Grove Flourishes

Once back in St. Augustine, Jack and Buckingham settled into a town much changed by the war. Jack revived his ministry, and Buckingham immersed himself in local affairs. He also carried on an extensive correspondence with his scholarly friends, such as Peter Force, George Bancroft, Jared Sparks, John Gilmary Shea, and others.

Together, Jack and his former master collaborated on making the orange grove into a showplace. Buckingham tested out new varieties of oranges and novel ways of cultivating them. The orange grove became a site favored by winter tourists for a delightful stroll and perhaps the treat of meeting Uncle Jack himself, who was usually much about. The poet and journalist William Cullen Bryant visited the grove in March 1873 after Buckingham's death and offered the following description in a letter to the *New York Evening Post*:

> One of the sights most worth seeing here is the place of the late Buckingham Smith . . . . The place is one of the finest things to be seen in East Florida. A lane between overhanging orange trees, now shining with their golden fruit, forming a fragrant covered way, leads to the mansion, which is overshadowed with giant mulberry trees. All around the mansion are rows of orange trees in full bloom, yet with their bright yellow fruit glittering here and there among the dark green, and scattered irregularly about are great gnarled fig trees, and pomegranate bushes put-

ting forth their green leaves. The dark color of the soil attests to the care which has been taken to enrich it with the dark mould of the marshes, and here and there you have the grateful feeling of treading upon an elastic turf formed by the vigorous growing grass, a sensation quite rare in Florida, where the grass of our northern region is almost a stranger. (Glicksberg 1936, 14(4):262–263)

More than marsh mud was responsible for the beauty of this oasis on the edge of town. On his many trips to Spain, Buckingham collected cuttings of various orange varieties to propagate in St. Augustine. An untitled four-page document on orange culture in Buckingham's handwriting found in the Buckingham Smith Collection demonstrates the scientific and painstaking method by which the grove came to its glory. A sentence in this document illustrates: "The ground was opened in two trenches 17 feet apart from the middle of each, the width of each 3 feet & the depth 2½ and were filled in with bone mixed thoroughly with decayed manure and earth" (Buckingham Smith, n.d.). The document continues with descriptions of grafting, transplanting, and cultivating, as well as coping with fungus and insect pests.

Buckingham was proud of his creation, bragging, "I have an orange avenue for which the ground was prepared in this way which visitors admire and travelers say they have not seen anything like abroad." Buckingham described how he formed the avenue:

Sour oranges, cut in quarters, were set in the trenches . . . in three seasons, if the grass be kept out, trees will make a show . . . by attraction the trees will meet above some 18 feet from the ground & without any teaching form a graceful gothic arch, and give a heavy shade. These trees may be budded with sweet orange but will of course not have the dark showy green of the Sevilla orange leaf. (Smith n.d.)

Buckingham was the planner, but Jack did the tedious tending, watering, fertilizing, and constant weeding needed to bring the avenue and the grove to perfection. By the end of his life, he knew as much or more about orange culture as Buckingham. Of course, he had no choice but to learn orange culture. However, he turned some of this horticulture to his advantage in his later years when he charged what one Yankee referred to as "exorbitant prices" for oranges from the grove.

Sketch of the "Orange Walk," carefully cultivated by Jack Smith on the Smith Estate. *Harper's New Monthly Magazine*, Harper & Brothers, New York, New York, December, 1874.

Buckingham's expression "gothic arch" speaks of a contemplative, religious air to the orange avenue. Ironically, when the avenue later became part of the Ball estate, it was called "lovers lane" because the unwarned might bite into a beautiful but sour orange. Subsequently, the avenue became part of Henry Flagler's Ponce de Leon Hotel grounds.

Jack's interest in the garden and grove is demonstrated by the number of pages in his narrative devoted to discussion of the plants that were introduced into St. Augustine during his many years in the town. He carefully mentions those responsible for the introduction and propagation of the plants, as this was an era of intense interest in transplantation and cultivation. Or was this emphasis in the narrative the result of Buckingham's

influence in the transcription? Dabbling in horticulture was considered a
gentleman's occupation in the nineteenth century. St. Augustine had its own
agricultural association with a membership that included prominent men in
town and wealthy planters. The association's focus was to experiment with
different and often exotic plants. For his part, Jack believed that few plants
remained to be cultivated in Florida other than those already brought in
colonial and early territorial times.

The two men began collaborating on Jack's narrative about four years after
they returned to St. Augustine from New York. No exact date for the writing is given, but clues from the narrative suggest that the year is probably
1869. Where the two sat to record the document is a mystery, although Jack
makes reference to his cabin in relation to the size of the elephant that he
saw in Africa. Were the two men working together in front of Jack's cabin?
One guesses that the narrative was not written in one sitting. The number of
changes and strikeovers in the story indicate some checking back and forth
as well as later corrections by Buckingham as he began to polish the narrative for publication. By then, Jack was officially credentialed as a Methodist
minister and Buckingham was in declining health. Circumstances and age
may have put both men in a mellow mood for review of their changed lives.

Legacy of the Smith Estate

Buckingham made several more trips during this time, including a last visit
to Spain and several to New York, where he toyed with the idea of taking up
permanent residence. While on a street in New York in January 1871, Buckingham collapsed as a result of apoplexy and heart problems. Unfortunately,
Jack was not with him in New York at that time. Buckingham's appearance—
being dressed in his usual slovenly way, one supposes—caused the authorities
to assume that he was a local drunk, so they put him in jail overnight to sober
up. The next day when it became obvious that he was not intoxicated but in
fact seriously ill, he was sent as a charity case to Bellevue Hospital. There he
died and was slated for burial in a pauper's grave until one of his New York
friends, a Mr. Williams, president of the Metropolitan Bank of New York,
discovered the body in the morgue and identified him. The body was then
shipped back to St. Augustine, where Buckingham was buried beside his wife

and mother in the Huguenot Cemetery, the Protestant burial ground just outside the city gate.

No will was found at first. Eventually, upon opening the safe of the local merchant, Burroughs Carr, who died several months before Buckingham, a proper document was found disbursing Buckingham Smith's holdings. At a time when no banks were yet established in St. Augustine, citizens customarily placed valuable documents in the safes of town merchants.

Jack was prominently featured in the will. In fact, Jack was the first legatee mentioned. He was granted the use of the orange grove for the remainder of his lifetime as well as life tenancy in the cabin. Jack was also willed all of Buckingham's clothes. Clothes were much more valuable in the nineteenth century before such items became mass-produced, and wills itemized clothing, bed linens, and dishware in great detail. Perhaps Buckingham's clothes needed to be made over for Jack. While Buckingham is described as a tall and portly man, Jack was just five feet and 135 pounds at the time of his death more than a decade later.

One hundred dollars were willed to each of the Smith family's former slaves: Judie (bought in Savannah), Binah, and Tina. Other items in Buckingham's possession, including some oil paintings, were distributed to his friends and relatives. A cottage scene by the artist Gainsborough was willed to a Maria Browne and a little picture of St. Francis was willed to the Catholic Church. Buckingham's books and papers were willed to the New York Historical Society (see Appendix D, "Buckingham Smith's Last Will and Testament").

The most substantial legacy, nearly the remainder of the estate, was left for the care of the "aged Negroes" of St. Augustine. This bequeath led to the establishment of the Buckingham Smith Benevolent Association, the first (and still existing) nonprofit charity in Florida. Since the money left was only about twenty-four thousand dollars, less than expected, some of Buckingham's friends contributed additional funds. A three-story nursing home facility was built on what is now Granada Street and later made into The Buckingham Hotel and, subsequently, torn down. Judie and several other former Smith slaves were given sanctuary there. The fund proved to be a lasting legacy in St. Augustine and still supports the care of elderly African-Americans in town.

Photograph circa 1870s of Home for Aged Negroes in St. Augustine built
by Buckingham Smith Benevolent Association. Photographic Collection,
St. Augustine Historical Society. By permission of St. Augustine
Historical Society, St. Augustine, Florida.

Jack was never a resident at the nursing home and continued occupying his cabin and working as usual in the orange grove more than a decade
longer. Henry Ball, who bought the Smith property, planned to build Jack
a porter's lodge near the entrance to the grove, but as far as we know, the
structure was never built. The double stereopticon images of Jack in front
of his cabin do not show anything as pretentious as a lodge, and his cabin
does not look new. Jack supported himself—along with contributions from
his parishioners—by selling oranges from his trees, picked fresh as groups of
tourists toured the grove, a popular pastime. Descriptions of him in his last
years give the impression that he was a quaint one-man tourist attraction, a
role he may have partly enjoyed because of the economic benefit.

By that time, the Anderson Grove to the south of the original Smith property was also much visited. The path from town where tourists strolled made
a Y, so they could promenade either way, but only near Jack's cabin did they
find an unusual guide, one so old and even born in Africa. In the years before

the 1875 article appeared in *Harpers New Monthly Magazine*, several hurricanes hit the town, resulting in the proposal to extend the sea wall on the waterfront or perhaps build an embankment on the Maria Sanchez Creek to cut down the chance of flooding. One woman was heard to remark, "I don't feel politically so much disturbed about the cost of the sea-wall ... if it keeps this grove from washing away. It is doing a sweet and noble duty in life ..." (Woolson 1875, L(296):171).

A Slave's View of Spanish St. Augustine

Jack began a whole section of the narrative by describing St. Augustine as he first saw it near the end of the Second Spanish period (1784–1821) of Florida's history. Memories of past times are tricky, and the difference in Jack and Buckingham's ages at the time being described affected the narrative as written. After all, Jack was a young adult at the end of Hispanic times while Buckingham was a young child. Likewise, the time factor was a problem for both. Their observations are impossible to fix into the short four-year time frame (1817–1821) as their reflections used the history of Spanish St. Augustine as a baseline that included the enduring Hispanic influence after Florida became a territory of the United States.

One pictures the two men sitting together with Buckingham asking Jack questions and partially filling in the narrative gaps with details from his own memory. The prose is at times more elaborate, reflecting Buckingham's hand in the description, but jumps back from time to time to the spare observational voice that is Jack's style. The description of Jack's entry by schooner into the St. Augustine harbor is characteristic of the poetic style of a nineteenth-century white gentleman of letters rather than a man of practical affairs, such as Jack. Take for instance this sentence: "The white

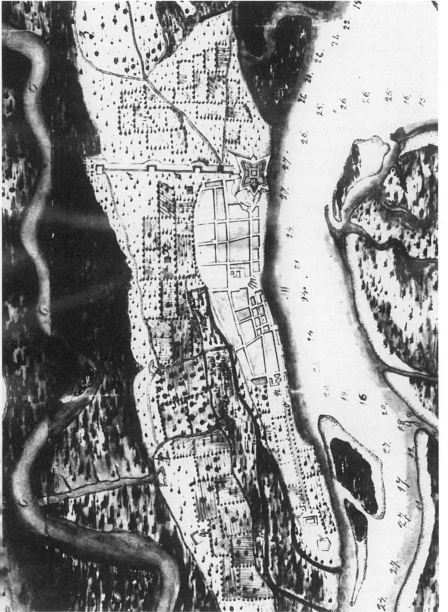

Ramon de la Cruz map of 1821, showing St. Augustine, area fortifications, and outlying fields. Map Collection, St. Augustine Historical Society. By permission of St. Augustine Historical Society, St. Augustine, Florida.

flat-roofed dwellings in the town were seated in groves, behind the bay of azure, over whence at this season a fragrance of orange blossoms [was] perceptible from our first drawing near the coast." Or again: "The sun went down leaving vivid colors spread over the western horizon beyond distant pine tops. A single drum rolls, and the flag on the castile [fort], a red lion in a yellow field floated for a moment in the air, and then came down from the staff."

For the remainder of the description of the town, the narrative seems to alternate between the narrator, Jack, and the recorder, Buckingham. Nevertheless, this section about St. Augustine is rich in descriptive detail, some of which is recorded nowhere else in the documentation on St. Augustine from the early part of the nineteenth century or, alternately, adds elements that elaborate on other known information.

Today, a trip down U.S. Highway 1 from Jacksonville to St. Augustine reveals a congested, rapidly urbanizing area. In contrast, once one is within the old section of St. Augustine, remnants of the early nineteenth-century town that Jack Smith described are evident on almost every corner: from the downtown plaza to the narrow streets with overhanging balconies to standing buildings from colonial times, especially the large fort looming on the bay front. Even the grid pattern of streets in the town's central area is much the same.

A Fortified Town

Not surprisingly, Jack's first description of the town notes its fortified aspect, as St. Augustine was a military town for centuries. Much of Jack's description is corroborated by the maps of the time. The town employed a circular perimeter extending from the fort, Castillo de San Marcos, to the Cubo Line to the north, on around to the Rosario Line on the west. This three-sided enclosure was referred to as a line of "circumvallation." According to Luis Arana, the line with its strategically placed redoubts (enclosed defensive structures) was altered and repaired constantly throughout the various time periods of St. Augustine's history (Waterbury 1999:187–210).

Jack particularly took note of the structure at the southernmost tip of the St. Augustine peninsula, referring to it as "*El Poso*" [the well]. Not a well at all, as it was positioned next to the saltwater marsh, *El Poso* was the nickname for the ruins of Fort Glazier, the seventh redoubt built in the shape of a pentagon during the British period. When the Second Spanish period began, it was renamed the Maria Sanchez Redoubt (Sastre 1990:53–93). Since the redoubts were made of palm logs, wood, sod, and sometimes coquina, they needed constant repair. By the end of the Second Spanish period, when the Smith family moved to town, the structure was almost completely demolished. By the time Jack saw it, the shape of what remained of the redoubt's interior resembled a well, hence the nickname. Opposite the military barracks, the sea wall (built in 1840) began and then continued back to the fort. Jack described the locations of several redoubts and mounted cannons. Not mentioned, however, were the Spanish bayonet plants (*yucca aloifolia* or *yucca baccata*). With long, stiff shoots ending in stiletto-like points, these plants were used on the earthworks as a barricade to the town.

The town plan and fortifications from the First Spanish period (1565–1763) generally followed the layout of the design established by the Spanish government for its colonies in the Americas. The scheme is somewhat elongated in St. Augustine, as the town occupies a long narrow peninsula. One change in Jack's time from early Spanish days was the transformation of the Monastery of the Immaculate Conception—the headquarters of the Franciscan Order in Florida during the First Spanish period—into a barracks to house soldiers in the Second Spanish period. Thus, Jack viewed the town as anchored at both ends by substantial military installations.

Some unknown or little known information is gleaned from Jack's description of the town's defensive layout. He described, for example, a secured entrance off the lot behind the Government House on the plaza: a "curtain" or section of the military fortification, as it is called, to protect the town from the west. The Maria Sanchez Creek, immediately behind the Government House, served as a moat on the other side of that curtain fortification. This seems to have been one of the few remaining sections of the Rosario Line near the end of the Second Spanish period. Since this part of the creek was filled in after the time of Jack's death, the southwest corner of the Government House is today at the intersection of Cathedral Place and Cordova Street.

We also gain otherwise unrecorded information about St. Augustine's city gate, also known as the Land Gate. Historian Luis Arana noted that "the gate consisted of two leaves hung on 2 strong masonry pillars" (Waterbury 1999:206). From his observation, Jack elaborated that the gates were "wood in two wings, the heels resting on stone and held erect by the staffs in rings of iron." The working mechanism is a rod-and-cups, bottom-and-top arrangement in accordance with old pictures of the gate that show a ring halfway up the inner coquina sides. This pattern is found on old fortified castles and forts in Europe, particularly in southern Spain where the Moorish influence prevailed.

Through the years, the military kept gunpowder in two structures—an old one and a new one—away from the Castillo [fort] to keep the powder dry, in Jack's opinion, and probably for safety. The Old Powder House was demolished by the time Jack dictated his narrative, but he remembered it well. In 1817, an orange grove flourished on the lot next to a two-room structure, which was converted into a dwelling after the new Powder House was built at the south end of town. The Old Powder House lot was at the head of the Maria Sanchez Creek on the west side of present Cordova Street and north of Jack's cabin. The specific description given of the window placement and large double doors fits the sketch drawn in 1867 by Henry J. Morton, titled the "oldest house in St. Augustine." Jack also noted that an attached kitchen with a fireplace was built when the structure was converted into a house. Graham, who edited and annotated the sketchbook, used Jack Smith's narrative to determine that the sketch was probably of the Old Powder House. As to its fate, an observer of St. Augustine writing in 1870 says that the house was torn down by "one Logan who was an army quarter-master... Mr. Logan used the stones of this unique ruin for his personal benefit" (Graham 1996:4–5; Woolson 1875, L(296):662).

The new Powder House was torn down at about the same time but not to be missed as, in Jack's eyes, it was ugly. Jack's description suggested a small replica of a fort with sentry boxes at each corner. It was made of thick stone in a parallelogram shape. The shingled roof that replaced the original tile was burned at some point, and the entire building became a sorry edifice. Placed near *El Poso*, the new Powder House probably also served as a guardhouse for protection of the city from any encroachment from the south. When Jack first saw the structure, it was guarded by a detachment of black soldiers.

Sketch circa 1867 of Old Powder House. Henry J. Morton Sketchbook,
St. Augustine Historical Society. By permission of St. Augustine Historical
Society, St. Augustine, Florida.

Soldiers and Townspeople

Jack presented a colorful picture-in-words of life in the plaza. At seven
o'clock, a bell on the nearby parish church announced the "*Oracion*," the
prayer section of the Catholic mass during which everyone stopped to pray.
Even the messenger in the street, carrying messages between the ramrod and
muzzle of his rifle, fell down to pray. Afterward, the occupants of the plaza
went about their ordinary business. Jack emphasized in the narrative how the
time of day, religious observances, and military security were interrelated.
Some of this is already known from other documentary sources; for example,
that the city gate was closed and locked at sundown and the key taken to the
Government House.

Adding to our understanding, Jack gave a more detailed picture of this
evening ritual. He described an elaborate guardhouse in the northeast corner
of the public square where a sentinel was stationed. Inside the guardhouse
was a place to detain delinquents in stocks. However, in addition to being

a jailer, the sentinel was also the town timekeeper. He used a "sand glass" to notify the townspeople of the time of day by striking each hour on the bell at the nearby market house. At nine o'clock in the evening, the bells chimed, notifying everyone of the curfew before the town was secured. Those caught out after that time and unable to answer the guard's challenge were incarcerated in the guardhouse until the next day. In Jack's account, we have the exact Spanish words of the challenge to those who were about the streets after this curfew, as well as the customary response given by those with legitimate business.

Question: "*Quien vive?*" [Who lives?]
Answer: "*España.*" [Spain]
Question: "*Que gente?*" [What people?]
Answer: "*Paisano.*" [Countryman]

In his narrative, Jack recorded an incident where a questionable response was given to this challenge. A man who had just recently been entertained by the governor was unable to give an account of himself; thus, he was locked in the guardhouse to the amusement of all who saw him the next morning. This anecdote gives a glimpse of the humor that was part of Jack's personality.

Intrigued with the Spanish regiment's presence in the town, Jack called them a "formidable force." Two companies from the second regiment of Cuba were present at the fort, and a company of mounted men occupied the Dragoon Lot on the western edge of the city not far from where Jack's cabin was built. In addition, an artillery company was stationed between the plaza and present day Artillery Lane. During the four years that Jack lived under the government of Spain, two regiments were also present: one Catalan and the other Malaga. These were crack outfits from Jack's description, as they had experienced battle in the Napoleonic Wars and overshadowed the soldiers from Cuba. However, one supposes that, with nothing to do, they indulged in some "excesses." Jack said that one of their number even challenged authority by sitting in the governor's chair in the Parish Church. Finally, their restlessness led to mutiny, and they escaped through the city gate to unknown destinations.

Of special interest to Jack were the two companies of "Negroes" stationed at the army barracks. They were charged with protecting the southern part of town as mentioned and were responsible for the redoubt near *El Poso*. Jack must have been heartened that they were "distinguished for their good conduct and subordination." Their captains were educated men, according to Jack's account, and traded at Josiah Smith's store. One of them taught Jack and his master how to bleach wax. If the wax in question was the locally made wax from the ubiquitous wax myrtle bushes growing around St. Augustine, it is a muddy color when first extracted from the berries. Wax, of course, was used for candles, sealing perishable foods, and waterproofing items. In St. Augustine, wax was also valued for tree grafting, particularly in the cultivation of orange trees.

In discussing the soldiers, Jack is specific in saying that they were served by two Franciscan friars as well as by the priest, Michael Crosby. Since he described the attire of the friars, "blue robes, sandals and very broad brimmed hats," one assumes that he saw them. This assumption argues against other documentation indicating that the Franciscans were out of the picture by that time, except for two who came in 1789. These two Franciscans were assigned to serve the Minorcan population, a Mediterranean group brought to Florida during the British period. Their priest, Dr. Pedro Camps, was ailing. The Franciscans proved ineffectual because they did not know the Minorcan language, so they stayed only a year (Gannon 1965:95).

Jack posed an additional puzzle in another section of his narrative manuscript discussing the Castillo, telling of "two friars of the order of St. Francis who [attended] the soldiery and after a year or two went to Cuba." Thus, we are left to wonder if the Franciscan presence in St. Augustine was more common at the end of the Second Spanish period than extant documents show. More likely, Jack mistook the Christian Brothers for Franciscans. Three Christian Brothers from Canada were recruited in 1858 to start a boy's school in the town. They stayed near the south end of Charlotte Street close to the barracks, but were gone by the time the Union troops captured the town in 1862 during the Civil War (Gannon 1965:168,173,184).

Buildings and Infrastructure

In addition to detailing the town's defensive fortifications, Jack undertook a description of individual buildings, monuments, roads, and bridges in St.

Augustine. Some of these still exist today, though often in modified form.
Jack described the roads open during his time in St. Augustine, personalizing
the account by recording that the extension of Treasury Lane "near which
I work with my hoe is [now] obliterated." The isolation of the town on the
land side is emphasized by his mention of the plank bridge that led across
Maria Sanchez Creek into the forest beyond, while "Picolata Avenue" leading to the St. Johns River was still, in 1817, a road of the future.

A monument stood in the center of the plaza—now referred to as Constitution Monument—which was erected near the end of the Second Spanish period. However, Jack spoke of it as having been built by the Spanish
and "raised to their constitution." This monument, built in the form of an
obelisk, was dedicated to the short-lived republican government active in
Spain for two periods between 1812 and 1823. Similar monuments were built
elsewhere in Spanish colonies overseas, but most such monuments were torn
down when the monarchy triumphed again. The one in St. Augustine remained because it was erected shortly before the Territorial period began,
so the U.S. government let it stand. Similar to tourists today, Jack evidently
did not know what to make of the square and compass near the base of the
monument. This Masonic symbol, now usually seen as a Protestant icon, was
a marker of liberal political and religious thought in Europe at that time. In
its brief tenure, the liberal government in Spain revived freemasonry from its
pre-Reformation Catholic form and temporarily suspended the Inquisition
(Ridley 2001:160–161).

Jack differentiated between the "better sort of people" and those of lesser
standing by reference to their houses. He noticed that those of affluence
lived in houses built of coquina stone, the shell/stone material quarried on
Anastasia Island. Coquina was also used to build the fort and most of the
public buildings. The better houses were regularly kept in acceptable shape
with lime wash, which was made with little effort at that time by burning
the ubiquitous oyster shells. In telling us that many of these houses were flat
roofed, we may conclude that second-stories were mostly added in the Territorial period (1821–1845) or even later.

In comparison, some of the smallest houses were cell-like, no more than
ten feet by ten feet at the smallest. These houses commonly followed the
form of European peasant dwellings, referred to as "Common Plan Houses."

Usually, they were constructed of wood and thatched with palm leaves and had one or two rooms, sometimes three. According to the Mariano de la Roque map of 1788 and accompanying building descriptions, about 70 percent of the houses in St. Augustine were of this type (Manucy 1962:49, 50–51; Roque 1788).

In subsequent years, many of these simpler houses fell into disrepair and did not survive. Often, as the houses were abandoned, the materials were carried off to build other structures; such was the fate of the old Powder House. Jack doubtlessly saw many such houses when he first viewed the town. In fact, his own cabin, built later, was of that form but sported a shingled roof, certainly better than the palm thatch that leaked in bad weather and often harbored insects and other vermin. Interestingly, Jack referred to his home as a "house" rather than a cabin. This reference is included in his comparison of the structure to the size of an elephant in Africa.

The principal buildings in the town are described in some detail. His description of the fort, its interior rooms and their functions, checks with other documentary sources of St. Augustine history. Jack mentioned the gradual destruction of the King's Chest, a money vault that dated back to the First Spanish period. Because St. Augustine was a remote outpost subject to both internal and external depredation, the cash reserves were kept at the fort. As Jack told it, the chest, which was kept in a heavily guarded room, was made of "solid wood, reinforced at the edges, bottom, and corners with iron, strongly barred and bearing three or four locks" (Bushnell 1981:1). Jack says that the King's Chest was secured with three locks (when he first saw it) and further explained that the "keys [were] severally in possession of the Governor, the Judge, and the Collector of the Port." However, he noted that even before the Civil War, chips were gouged out of the wood from time to time, perhaps by tourists or curiosity seekers, until the King's Chest no longer existed.

Other civil depredations and natural events also took their toll. The Castillo de San Marcos has a long history and has undergone periodic deterioration with subsequent repair. In 1817, when Jack first saw the fort, it was in disrepair, partly because the Spanish loss of Florida to the United States was imminent; thus, the cost of repair was not considered justified. The corner of the fort's southeast bastion [jutting out to allow crossfire] had fallen into the sea, the glacis [sloping embankment to the moat] was dug away on its north side, and some interior structural parts were "crumbled." Even today, under the auspices of the National Park Service, the fort needs to be refurbished from time to time as wind and weather, along with a settling of the walls, takes its toll.

While the financial reserves were stored in the King's Chest at the fort, the Customs House near the bay front handled the day-to-day collection of monies and the accounting for the province in the Second Spanish period. What Jack referred to as "the edifice of the revenue" was not the building where the accounts were rendered, although it was known as the "Treasurer's House" for many years. This building is still standing at the southeast corner of Treasury and St. George Street, owned now by the city but operated by the Women's Exchange. The longstanding misnomer for this house results from its use as a residence by Juan Estevan de Pena, the Royal Treasurer in the First Spanish period, although his treasury business was conducted elsewhere. In later periods of St. Augustine's history, the building continued as a private residence. The Peck family, for example, lived there a long time. Like the Smiths, they were from Connecticut but came to St. Augustine in 1833, somewhat later than the Smith family. Dr. Seth Peck attended to the Smith family and their slaves, including Jack. Later, his son John, a medical doctor, also attended to them.

The Peck House was somewhat of a ruin when Jack first saw it. The house was renovated many times, including the addition of an upper story, though an attached floor to the east may have been the base of another structure. When the house was still one story, it had an unusual feature: down spouts in the form of small canons. This kind of down spout, usually made of clay, was commonly used in St. Augustine, as in Spain, to drain the flat roofs of one-story houses. The narrative is vague as to whether Jack only heard of this feature or whether it was still on some St. Augustine houses in the early nineteenth century.

Many people even today mistake this house as the Royal Treasury building in Spanish times, but it is odd that Jack made this mistake. Moreover, one would think that Buckingham might have known otherwise. Jack does mention the Custom House in describing the importation and exportation of town goods, but one assumes that he believed the actual accounting was done in the Treasury Street building.

Sketch of Government House, 1764—note the pilasters, later made into benches. Collection, St. Augustine Historical Society. By permission of St. Augustine Historical Society, St. Augustine, Florida.

An elaborate standing wall on St. George Street was across from the "Trea- surer's House." Jack thought that the wall might have been originally part of a house. He notes the impressive pilasters (flattened pillars attached to a wall). The window apertures (openings) had iron bars. A writer in *Harpers New Monthly Magazine* implied that the wall was actually part of the Royal Treasury building, while a contemporary guidebook indicates that it was an unfinished house. It could also have been an elaborate garden wall. Henry J. Morton pictured this wall in his 1867 sketchbook with the caption, "wall face to a garden—Spanish." Being familiar with the Spanish tradition from his years in Spain, Buckingham probably suggested the garden wall to Jack as an explanation. In any event, this mystery wall was torn down in 1877.

Jack is particular in noting features of the "Governor's House," now called Government House, which stands in reconstructed and modified form on the west end of the central plaza. What Jack saw was a house of two stories on its east side with an attached one story with a flat roof on its west side. He added the droll touch that the pillars (actually pilasters) were removed from the outside stairway on the east and ended up as benches under the nearby fig trees. Little details such as this add piquancy to Jack's account. Jack implied that the smithy shop with its stone construction and arched windows was an imposing edifice. The site of the original smithy is now under Highway A1A near the fort.

Churches and Cemeteries

Two buildings on each side of the plaza were of religious interest to Jack. The Catholic Church to the north was the only religious facility in use when Jack first came to St. Augustine. East Florida, as a Catholic Spanish province, was a theocracy at the time. Jack did not give a description of the outside of the church, but then little description is needed. The church, now known as the Cathedral Basilica of St. Augustine, still stands in the same location today. Jack was more fascinated with the human behavior associated with the church. As he tells us, people raised their hats as they passed by the church portal. The church was also a welcome temporary sanctuary for criminals, as was the custom at that time. Jack captured a view of the inside of the church that evokes an actual visit to a mass. The words are explicit, "At church, tags and ribbons fluttered from the candelabra, incense rose before the altar, then from a silver censor; music vocal and instrumental proceeded from the gallery, and the women seated on the several rugs upon the *tabi* floor counted their rosaries in prayer, and flashed their [tasseled?] fans." All our senses are engaged as we read this description. We are also given a brief insight into the status rankings, age, and gender mix of the townspeople from the seating arrangements in the church. We know from Jack's account that the men sat around the walls on two rows of benches, the women sat on the floor, and the governor had a special chair that was positioned nearest the altar. These descriptions by Jack are unique and valuable additions to our knowledge of the parish church and its interior during the Second Spanish period and beyond. Significant in its absence is any mention by Jack of the seating arrangements for black parishioners, although other documentary sources disclose that persons of color were required to stay in a separate gallery. This gallery was reached by a staircase near the church entry.

We also learn about the colors of mantillas, the women's head scarves worn in church and at different times of the day: white for morning mass and black for later in the day. Other references to the women's headwear only mention black; presumably, the other writers of the time did not go to the early mass. The early service, as we know from other documents, attracted mostly women, their children, and old people. The men were off at work by that time so the women of the town used the time after mass to visit with each other before they began the day's work.

The second building of religious interest to Jack was across the street, although its remains were barely visible in 1817. Jack was told that it was an English Church but, in actuality, its history was more complicated. A remarkable piece of research by Elsbeth Gordon reveals that the building was built in the early 1700s during the First Spanish period and was referred to as the "palacio Episcopal" [bishop's house], where Bishop Francisco de San Buenaventura lived until 1745. In the British period, the building was briefly used as a church, then occupied by British troops, and finally renovated extensively and enlarged into a British statehouse with two newly constructed end sections. The British were proud of this building. Its newly altered form was elaborate in the neoclassic style, and the building even included a theatre. The impressive nature of the edifice clearly shows that the British did not foresee that they would lose Florida. Later, during the Second Spanish period, the once-imposing building fell into ruin, as Jack observed when the Smith family moved to St. Augustine. Trinity Episcopal Church was eventually built in the same location, probably using part of the foundation or other original materials (Gordon 2002:103–110).

In Jack's narrative, the three cemeteries of the time are given exact placement in the town, which is of special interest to archaeologists or others who in later times confirmed these locations by finding bodies or other grave materials. He named three cemeteries: the Tolomato cemetery, which was Catholic and is still preserved today in the northwestern section of St. Augustine; the cemetery at the south end of town; and an early cemetery just to the south of the plaza. Jack also called to our attention some evidence that the British, too, used the Tolomato cemetery for burial. His evidence is slim on this but intriguing, as the cemetery at the south end of town is actually designated as the English cemetery. Also, Protestants were sometimes buried on Anastasia Island at El Vergel ("the garden" or "the grove"). A good guess is that burials of the English in the Tolomato cemetery during Spanish times were probably Catholics of Anglo-Celtic descent who converted to Catholicism. For example, the well-known St. Augustine Welsh woman, Mary Evans, converted to Catholicism toward the end of her life and was buried in Tolomato cemetery (CPR 1784–1809, 1:129). Other documents have made clear that bodies were buried in shallow graves—only two and a half or three feet under—and complaints were raised in the Second Spanish period about the smell from the Tolomato cemetery when the wind blew from the west during warm weather.

The Marketplace and Trade

The old market building, which still stands at the east end of the plaza, had at that time a low one-story latticed building attached to it where meat was sold. On the building's west side hung the city bell. Inside the market, "the material belonging to the King's launch that gave pilotage across the bar" was stowed. South of that location was the King's apothecary, *la botica*. The vegetable and fish markets were to the south and east of these two buildings.

Jack provided this valuable information on the layout of the market and also describes in detail what was offered for sale. Beef and pork were the main meats sold, although the beef was not stall fed, which may indicate an inferior quality. As might be expected, Jack was interested in the experiments in raising sheep. The governor had a well-bred stock, but they were worried by the dogs in town. Although Jack gave the dogs as the reason, we know today that sheep do not do well in warm, damp climates, such as St. Augustine.

Fish, of course, given St. Augustine's location, was a mainstay: "plenty and cheap," as Jack noted. He added the exact dimensions of the tables, "4 ft. square," where fish were sold. The vegetables, he thought, were better than in later times, such as the chiote [in the squash family] that grew on arbors in the town. Tomatoes were still eaten at that time, this being before the era when they were called "love apples" and thought to be poisonous. Jack relished the sweet pepper, which was roasted, skinned, and covered with oil. Vendors roamed about selling honey in the comb. They sold fruits from baskets on their heads—figs, grapes, peaches, and oranges. Other vegetables were sold from baskets, particularly the "tania" and "vio." Both tania and vio are roots—varieties of the elephant ear plant—which are much eaten in the West Indies. Thus, Jack's account provides knowledge of foodstuffs used in

Photograph of painting circa 1840 of plaza in St. Augustine, showing boat basin, market buildings, Constitutional Monument (center), and churches. Photographic Collection, St. Augustine Historical Society. By permission of St. Augustine Historical Society, St. Augustine, Florida.

St. Augustine that are not specifically mentioned in other documents. Other sellers hawked shrimp by the plateful for six cents and oysters by the quart at the same price. Stone crabs were harvested from the coquina rocks at the northern tip of Anastasia Island and at Matanzas on the southern tip of the island.

The Seminole Indians who came into town to trade added to the colorful scene. They came from west of the St. Johns River and from the Alachua section of Florida in the vicinity of what was later the town of Gainesville. Other observers have enumerated the goods traded at the time, but Jack furnished an extensive list. According to him, among the goods that Indians brought to town for sale were beeswax, wild honey, snakeroot, bear's oil, raw and dressed deerskins, wild turkeys, and deer. They also engaged in slave trafficking, bringing slaves for sale in the town.

Sometime around 1810, black slaves became part of the Seminole Indian settlement configuration. They can be divided into two types: first, those who ran away from the plantation or another location, and second, those who were captured by the Seminoles in raids. The runaways were valued, given their freedom, and some were settled in satellite—often defensive—towns outside the tribal centers. The black slaves who were captured became slave labor and could be expendable if money was needed or if they proved to be intractable. Presumably, no questions were asked by the white purchasers. The black issue became a contributing factor in the Second Seminole War.

The Indians traded their goods for powder, lead, homespuns, shrouds, beads, pocket looking glasses, combs, worsted bindings, and carmines for face painting. Other documents of the time tell of the Indians who, having consumed too much alcohol on market days, could be found lying under the shade of the street-side balconies.

Questionable or unpleasant happenings are absent in the narrative, although such were certainly observed. Jack told of some Indians who "lingered late about the town" and went outside the town foraging for huckleberries, palmetto fruit, and dry sticks to sell for fuel. He does not mention that the reason for Indians overstaying was drunkenness, a result of the alcohol traded to them by the white men, a practice documented in other sources. Jack also chose not to tell of the Indian troubles and war that disrupted the town in the many years he spent in St. Augustine. For example, Indians were marauding in the countryside as early as 1800. Jack's narrative also omits any reference to the cataclysmic Second Seminole War, which greatly affected the town in 1835. In the same year that Indian trade in St. Augustine was brought to a standstill, the orange groves suffered a severe freeze that wiped out many trees.

Both edible and ornamental plants were of interest. Buckingham, like other white gentlemen of the day living in exotic environments (as Florida was considered at the time), was much engaged in introducing and experimenting with various plants. As his collaborator, Jack was charged with the day-to-day planting and care of these plants. In telling of plant varieties, Jack said that "it is worthy of reflection how small has been the addition to the fruits and vegetables that were grown here by the Spaniards." Evidently, he was of the opinion that most of the plants from the Antilles and Mexico were introduced in the First Spanish period. He named the wild banana and the loquat as exceptions and mentioned the men who introduced them. Nevertheless, he identified other new cultivars introduced during the years after the American period began. Among these, he adds the Ishia [Smyrna] fig, the yam from Georgia in the early 1800s, the white potato introduced later, the malaga grape, the hardy scuppernong grape, and the tangerine or whether the reference was to mariposa lillies.

The men who introduced these varieties were associated with the late days of Spanish hegemony and the early days of U.S. hegemony, such as Jephaniah Kingsley, whom Jack first heard of in Africa. Surprisingly, not mentioned was that Buckingham Smith himself brought varieties of oranges from Spain to try in Florida. Buckingham's initiative probably accounted for the show-place quality of the orange grove. In speaking of the oranges—which were the main source of revenue for the town prior to a devastating freeze in the early to mid-nineteenth century—Jack describes the seasonal scene. Oranges were picked early in October and November and then transported across the plaza to the boat basin, where they were shipped to ports from Charleston to New Haven.

The market trade on the plaza was the main sphere of interaction for the townspeople. The town plaza was also the gateway to the outer world. The imported goods were carried in wheelbarrows or, in the case of barrels, rolled to the Custom House. Imports from the "American ships" included soap, flour, tobacco, and blue homespuns. Although some trade with Charleston took place, Jack named Havana as the principal trade partner of the town in the Spanish regime. Annually, during Spanish colonial times, ships entered the harbor providing money and troops to St. Augustine. The periodic ship-ment of money to support the town, the *situado*, was the continuing assis-tance for what, at best, was a minor metropolis, considered by the Spanish authorities as a necessary military outpost for the empire (Bushnell 1994). By the end of the Second Spanish period, this annual shipment of funds was sporadic and usually short of the requested amount.

Jack named a number of Havana imports in the narrative, including beans, "Veracruz peppers," saffron for soups, sweetmeats, wines, rum, and olive oil. Non-edible items of remark were the linens and fine fabrics. On the return voyage to Cuba, cardinals and mocking birds—captured in the spring, kept in palmetto cane cages, and taught "Spanish airs"—were in-cluded in the cargo. Jack was aware of this small venture; but, as he told it, after the bird incident in Connecticut, he could never afterward capture or kill a bird. Curiously, the *mariposas* [butterflies] are noted on a separate piece of paper accompanying the narrative. One wonders whether butterflies were also captured and sold.

The only flower Jack mentioned was the "Spanish pink" (a variety of the carnation), which was recorded as common in the town by many other observers. Jack was fascinated by the fact that none grew on the ground; instead, all were kept in pots on the balconies that overhung the narrow streets. Perhaps these pinks with their pungent aroma were an antidote to the overwhelming odors of dung and garbage as well as cooking smells drifting from open windows and yards. Other odors may have been worse. Sometimes a family proudly displayed a deceased relative on a homemade bier outside on the street, even in hot weather, so that passersby could admire the spectacle (Bemrose 1966:11).

Celebrations, Etc.

Jack described the people of earlier times as "the gayest I can imagine, celebrations following one after the other the year around." His description of these gala celebrations is consistent with those described by another man who wrote of them at exactly the same time, an anonymous English adventurer who was then in St. Augustine and Fernandina (Anonymous 1819:163–164). Both men described the balls, serenades, processions, and masquerades that took place, particularly at the time of Carnival. These festivals were tied to the seasonal rounds of agricultural activity in the Mediterranean. The St. Johns Day Carnival was celebrated at the end of the year's harvest on the Spanish island of Minorca. Jack particularly noted the carnival in June that preceded St. Johns Day. Most of these celebrations and festivals were part of the Catholic tradition brought from the Mediterranean in the late eighteenth century by the Minorcans. The other writer also observed the larger scale pre-Lenten carnival marking the beginning of the growing season (Griffin 1991).

While he does not speak of the change, Jack lived long enough to know of the abrupt end of the St. Johns Day celebration. Early in the Church's colonization efforts in the Americas, the Catholic authorities in Rome named eight celebrations that were to be dropped from the liturgical calendar in the colonial Americas because they were based on early pagan celebrations.

St. Johns Day was one of these. The festival had been grafted onto the pagan celebration of Midsummer Night's Eve at the time of the summer solstice, a time of frivolity and sexual license. In St. Augustine, as in many other places, this prohibition was ignored for many years. However, after many years of lay leadership, Augustin Verot was named Bishop of St. Augustine in 1858 and set about correcting a number of abuses, including the celebration of St. Johns Day and the attendant carnival (Taylor, M. D. 1916; Gannon 1965:28). As a result, the pre-Lenten and St. Johns Day Carnival gradually disappeared, although parts of the celebration lasted until the end of the nineteenth century.

Sunday after mass in St. Augustine was a convivial time for Catholics, with amusements and market activity. Incoming Protestants later decried these local practices as evidence of Catholics' lack of proper solemnity on the Sabbath. Jack further noted that "the recreation of sea bathing began on St. John's Day." Remarked on were the children's games: marbles, tops, and kites. In recent times, archaeologists have found marbles and tops in colonial contexts (Waters 2004). The games mentioned were usually boys' games. Here, Jack does not tell us if the slave or free black boys were engaged in these activities along with the white children. Nevertheless, as children often play together regardless of race or ethnicity, he may have seen boys, both white and black, engaging in these games together.

In describing the clothes worn by the men and women, Jack observed simple hunting shirts of checked cotton, palmetto hats from Havana, and moccasins for the men. The women wore "a silk slip" (meaning a dress), a mantilla, and shoes they made for themselves, which were cotton for everyday and satin for festive occasions. He saw no bonnets on the women, except for one made of beaver. Parasols were embellishments that came later. He must have been describing the dress of the white inhabitants, as etchings in the 1800s and later photographs depict slightly different clothes for the black women, who wore full skirts overlain with aprons and cloth bandanas on their heads.

Most activity about town was done on foot. Sometimes "tackeys" were used with "beef carts," as Jack called them. Tackeys were unkempt and shaggy looking small horses thought to be descendants of an Andalusian breed brought to Florida in the First Spanish period. They were in use in St. Au-

gustine until the beginning of the twentieth century and a few went wild on
Anastasia Island, which led to their other name, "marsh ponies." These carts
were often yoked to oxen as well and used for hauling. According to documents and photographs, the ox rig and cart continued in use in the town and
countryside until the end of the nineteenth century, past the time of Jack's
death. On first coming to town, Jack noticed only one substantial vehicle,
the "one-horse chaise" belonging to the Treasurer. Later, four-wheeled carriages and Jersey wagons were brought from New York and sold in the Smith
mercantile establishment. With these conveyances, passengers were taken to
the mouth of Pablo Creek to meet the boat coming from St. Marys. The mail
also came this way, brought once a week by mounted dragoon. This route
was probably the one that the Smith family took into town when they first
moved to St. Augustine in 1817.

Beyond the Town

Jack adds to his picture of the town the description of another nearby neighborhood across the bay to the east at the northern tip of Anastasia Island,
known as "south beach." There we find the watchtower—precursor to the St.
Augustine Lighthouse—and the fortifications downriver at the Matanzas
Inlet. Jack admitted that he had never visited Matanzas. He obviously visited
or observed the watchtower nearby, as he depicts its wooden arms that could
be raised either north or south to indicate the direction from which a vessel was approaching the town. In subsequent years, he saw the watchtower
gradually crumbling into the sea.

    Also on Anastasia Island was Jesse Fish's plantation. In Spanish days, the
Fish plantation was known as "El Vergel." Today, we know this as Fish Island,
although the land is not actually surrounded by water. Jack described the
remains of the former orange groves there, the house next to the huge date
palm tree, and the gravestone marking the burial site of Fish's son. While
riding on horseback, the son and his horse were killed by a bolt of lightning
on August 18, 1812. Jessie Fish Sr. is probably also buried at this location, although Jack does not mention it in his narrative. In fact, Jack seems to have
misunderstood, because he implied that the grave was where the elder Fish
was buried.

Farther north on Anastasia Island was another house and more trees. Jack notes the "elevation thrown up by [General James] Oglethorpe" where a battery fortification of cannons was placed as part of the siege of St. Augustine. This failed British siege, engineered by the Georgia colony to the north, took place in 1740 during the First Spanish period.

After mentioning that two shot holes dating to that siege could be seen in the east side of the fort, he took note of the fields north of the city gate and fort. There, sweet potatoes and corn were cultivated, but no trees or buildings other than huts were permitted in order to allow "the free play of cannon, should occasion require." This open space covered 1,500 Spanish yards and stretched to the woods called "*Mil y Quinientos*." According to Jack, this defensive area was farmed with low-growing plants by the Minorcans who lived south of the city gate near what Jack referred to elsewhere as "Minorcan town," a barrio section of the Spanish city.

The Minorcans were a large group of Mediterraneans brought to Florida in 1768 during the British period (1763–1783) to farm an indigo plantation seventy miles south of St. Augustine at New Smyrna. Most of the group fled to St. Augustine in 1777 because of many problems on the plantation, including harsh treatment by the onsite proprietor and his overseers and the uncertainties of the Revolutionary War times. The Minorcans settled in the north section of St. Augustine and were allowed to cultivate farm plots north of the city gate. They remained for many years as the major part of the white population of the town. Their descendents can still be found in St. Augustine and Florida today (Griffin 1991).

Fort Mose, spelled phonetically as "Moosa" in the narrative, was a settlement to the north of St. Augustine. The fortification and its attached village was developed as a sanctuary for runaway slaves from the lower South who sought their freedom in Florida during the First Spanish period. Jack devoted some space later in his narrative to describing the Sunday picnics that took place on the ruins of Fort Mose. He referred to these picnics with the Spanish word *convites*, meaning "picnics." According to his observation, the gentlemen (another version of the manuscript notes "citizens") of the town rode out on tackeys to the ruins of Fort Mose. On the day before the picnic, brushwood was collected in anticipation of cooking the picnic food. A "negro" brought piles of oysters in a canoe to the nearby landing. On the day of the picnic, the oysters were roasted and dressed with oil, sour orange juice, and "*ajo*" [garlic], and then the whole tasty morsel was washed down with Catalan wine. Jack summed up the jolly occasion, remarking that "the little cost and sobriety of these entertainments would astonish now." This unique and lively vignette in Jack's narration, found in no other documents, is a historical gem.

Changes Over Time

Jack had the impression that the number of people was greater when he first entered St. Augustine than fifty years later when he was recording his impressions. His observation was accurate. At the time of his arrival, the town was bustling. In contrast, after the Civil War when he was dictating his memoirs, the town was distressed, having been largely Confederate in persuasion but occupied by Union troops during most of the Civil War. In this excursion into earlier times, Jack told of the small farmers and planters who left the state after 1835 (Griffin 1999). He referred to seeing the blacks who lived and cultivated their vegetable crops outside of town. They were left over from the colony of free blacks at Fort Mose remaining from the First Spanish period. He referred also to the number of "English," as he calls them (left over from the British period), whose plantations stretched from the St. Marys River along the St. Johns River and on to the area of Cape Canaveral.

After the Civil War, the population fell to low ebb, and many of those who remained were impoverished. The flow of tourists was virtually nonexistent. Jack's observation of the town in 1869, of course, does not foretell of the population increase in subsequent decades. Those years were particularly explosive in growth, beginning with what became known as the Flagler Era (1885–1914). Several years after Jack's death, Henry Morrison Flagler filled in the northern section of Maria Sanchez Creek, paved streets, and then built elaborate hotels and other buildings, altering the configuration of the western edge of town. We thus have from Jack's account a picture of the village that St. Augustine was before this large-scale developer undertook the effort to urbanize the community and attract elite tourists.

After Jack's long description of the town, he made an obvious transition in the narrative. Following his remarks about changes in St. Augustine over time, and especially changes in the inhabitants, he added a thoughtful comment: "I am no less sensible of the changes that have come over me." Then he introduced a change in the narrative by saying, "I return to speak of myself."

V

ON BECOMING A FREEDMAN

As Methodist Minister in St. Augustine

Jack's spiritual and religious experiences enriched the last fifty-nine years of his life. As a Methodist preacher and later as a credentialed minister, he was in a position to be a leader of his people. Although Jack spent a good part of his life as a Christian, Jack's family background was Muslim. The religion of his father impressed him enough as a young child that, in his narrative, Jack included a description of his father at prayer. He remembered his father with his head touching the ground, uttering the words of the five-times-a-day prayer to Allah.

At the time, Sitiki was too young to attend the school where instruction was given in the Muslim religion and Arabic language. This brief exposure at an early age was not enough to ensure that he would adhere to the religion of his father, as many slaves did once they reached American shores. In fact, he was probably not exposed to Islam in any significant way after he left the family hearth. More likely, he became aware of the "religion of Guinea" in its indigenous African pagan form as practiced in St. Augustine. In his extensive archeological investigations in the city, Karl Halbirt, city archaeologist of St. Augustine, found chicken burials. All were articulated (jointed), and some were planted upright and missing their heads, indicating a form of ritual sacrifice that is common in pagan ceremonies in West Africa and the West Indies (Landers 1999:132–133; Metraux 1959:171–173).[1]

During the Second Spanish period, even white Protestants—although able to own property—were not allowed to practice their religion openly. The Spanish authorities were particularly worried about proselytizing among the slaves. Yet, Jack was not the first black man to preach the Methodist gospel to his fellows. In July 1815, a complaint was filed by a number of plantation owners south of St. Augustine concerning the conduct of a freedman named Antonio Williams, referred to as an "Anabaptist of Methodist faith." Williams was reported preaching to the slaves and exhorting them to escape from their masters. When the case was heard, Williams declared that he was not guilty but that another Antonio from a nearby plantation was the culprit. The court, unable to sort out the conflicting testimony, was somewhat lenient with Williams since he was a cooper (a barrel maker) and an excellent workman. He was not put in jail but was required to leave East Florida. The master of the other Antonio was requested to sell him (EFP 1785–1823, Microfilm Reel 126, #5). The case was settled just before the Smiths moved to St. Augustine. The local attitude began to change five or six years later when Florida became a U.S. territory and a missionary field opened for Protestants.

For his part, Jack showed little interest in religion in his early years. The first religious feeling that he experienced came when he was about sixteen years old, probably about the time that the Smiths moved to St. Marys, Georgia. He asked the searching question, "Why can I too not go to heaven? I do not swear, I do not steal, I keep no bad company." A couple of years later "in coming to live among the Spaniards," Jack reported the waning of any religious feeling. One can only guess at the reason for this: perhaps culture shock at a foreign way of life; more likely the influence of the Protestant Smith family. Even though he does speak of the religious celebrations of the Catholics in town in a somewhat positive way, he may have had some uncomfortable experiences with Catholicism as practiced by the Spanish and Minorcan populace that he did not want to mention.

Later, he reached another period of spiritual questioning. After asking himself some more probing questions, he "retired into the bush and prayed."

He also "read something," although he does not tell us the nature of his reading. Since he did not learn to read until after he came to St. Augustine, much of this soul searching must have taken place there.

The big break in Jack's religious experience came in 1823, when he was perhaps thirty years old, six years after moving to St. Augustine. At that time, he converted to Methodism under the tutelage of the Reverend Joshua Nichols Glenn. During Spanish days, Florida was—at least in name—a Catholic theocracy, but after the change of flags in 1821, ministers of various Protestant denominations arrived in St. Augustine and began scrambling for converts, bumping into each other in the process. Glenn was sent as a missionary to the town after being chosen for that station at the annual session of the South Carolina Methodist Conference. A native of Jackson County, Georgia, he and his two brothers all became Methodist ministers (Glenn 1945:121–123).

Without a Protestant church building in town, the Protestant missionaries and ministers of the various denominations and their congregations met in the "Council House Chambers," the building now called Government House at the west end of the plaza. Sometimes, they met singly with their congregations; other times, they assembled for joint meetings referred to as the Bible Society. Ralph Waldo Emerson, a recently ordained Unitarian Minister, came to St. Augustine for his health in 1827 and was appalled by these meetings. As a New Englander, he found the preaching and atmosphere far from dignified, even to the point of a fight breaking out one Sunday. He was especially amazed at the "unmannerly conduct" of a Methodist minister whom he referred to as "Mr. Jerry," doubtlessly the Rev. John L. Jerry, who seemed to have been in and out of the city during the early years of the Territorial period (Emerson 1827).

The Reverend Glenn's proselytizing among the white citizens of St. Augustine was far from successful. From his diary, which was written in his inimitable writing and spelling style, he appears to have been a rather rigid and opinionated fellow who invoked the books of Corinthians to admonish his would-be converts. He frequently went head-to-head with other Protestant ministers in town. In his diary, Glenn described a sermon that he gave when Andrew Fowler, the popular Episcopal clergyman, was in the audience. He chastised Fowler and another clergyman, noting that they "go to balls, card partys *and do worse* [emphasis his] then preach to the people that it is no harm and try to prove it from the Scripture." Ultimately, he tangled with Parson Eleazar Lathrop, the Presbyterian minister with whom he shared the meetinghouse. An attempt was made by Lathrop and others to prevent Glenn from holding worship services in that location. Although the plan failed, the tenuous balance among the Protestant ministers in town was altered (Glenn 1945:135–139).

Several white Spanish Catholics did attend services as a novelty and "seemed charmed with [the] singing and prayer," until they were threatened with excommunication by the Catholic priests (Laney 1825:113). Glenn made much better progress with the blacks. His hearty and vigorous preaching and willingness to have them shout and otherwise express their exuberance in church was an attraction. For a southerner in that era, he seems to have been less prejudiced than most white ministers. He was following the missionary thrust of the Methodist Church in the southern United States, whose primary interest was in converting slaves and freedmen in the newly open missionary field of Florida (Brooks, W. E. 1965:17–18).

When Noah Laney arrived in December 1823 to relieve Glenn of his missionary duties, he was amazed that "our coloured members in this place seem very pious. Indeed I never saw so promising a society of blacks, so much devoted to God. They hold communion with Him, and walk in the light of His countenance. So evident is the change in their conduct, that it is remarked on by the people here as something extraordinary" (Laney 1825:113).

Josiah Glenn's black converts, including Jack, cared for him as his physical health deteriorated and mental depression brought him close to the brink of suicide. He admitted in his diary entry of May 31, 1823, that he was "Sometimes allmost temted to wish I was out of the world" (Glenn 1945:139). He was in better spirits by the time that Jack's name appeared in his diary. The entry for Sunday, October 5, 1823, noted: "in the evening baptized a black man by the name of Jack who joined our Society heare." In the tally of converts at the end of the diary, Glenn listed the entry: "Oct 5 . . . Jack . . . age 30 . . . owner Smith's—free Jan 18" (Glenn 1945:151,158). As an aside, the last part of the entry is puzzling, as no evidence has been found that Jack was manumitted at that time, but this notation could refer to Jack's recognition of Jesus as his savior who spiritually set him free.

Jack himself does not mention his baptism. Instead, he says that his first religious instruction was from Glenn and that he "joined the church and took the sacrament on the 26th of December." Jack might have been particularly enthusiastic about the "love feast" that Glenn conducted on December 20. Love feasts in the old Methodist tradition were closed-door meetings, usually held quarterly, to express love for God and for one another. Testimonials were welcome (Wheeler 1886:129). The love feast conducted by the Reverend Glenn became an emotional outpouring, such that "love flowed into our souls and shouts of praise filled the house." Glenn also confided to his diary, "one poor African [Jack] got up and after telling of how he was brought away from his country and how he got on Since and the way he first came to heare me preach as also the manner of his conviction & conversion all of which he done in a few words—he then added—'and now if my Massa would give me my freedom and all Augustine I would not turn my back from my religion'" (Glenn 1945:156).

The Rev. Laney, who was also present at the love feast, reported the same story but supposedly in the exact words of the slave—almost surely Jack—who spoke feelingly: "Oh . . . I once hate God—no love his people—I was sinner—but when I came and hear de gospel I was convinced I was wrong. Oh, I now love God—his people—me love Jesus—he sinner's friend—and, O if my massa was to give me all Augustine, I would not turn back"(Laney 1825:113). Laney continued in explanation, "this poor man was born in Africa, and never heard the name of Jesus until he came to America. He is now a happy Christian." This reported assertion on Jack's part that he would not trade in his religion for his freedom seems to be a comment made in an exuberant moment with the knowledge that this was a choice he would never face.

Although Glenn left St. Augustine after a year, Jack remained a Methodist for the remaining years of his life. Somewhat later, Jack and Caleb Simmons, a black Presbyterian, practiced reading the Bible chapter by chapter. The two also took reading lessons from Elias B. Gould, the editor of the *East Florida Herald* and a dedicated Presbyterian, who established the first "Calvinist Sunday School" in Florida in 1822.

At first, in the Methodist mission effort, whites and blacks attended the same services. As time went on, whites met in the morning and blacks in the afternoon or at night. Two maps show the "Methodist Meeting House," as it was sometimes called, located on Charlotte Street in the second block north of the plaza. No dimensions are given, but it appears small. The church was built in 1829 at the time that Isaac Boring, a white man, occupied the pulpit.

The city passed an ordinance at about that time to decrease the chance of collusion in planning a riot. The ordinance required a white person to be present at each black church service. Once, when no white adult could fulfill this role, an amusing incident occurred. Julia Axtell, a white girl no more than six years old, was sent in place of her father, an Episcopal clergyman who suddenly took ill and could not attend. Questions were raised, but on examination, the authorities determined that the girl had fulfilled her duty properly (Kirk 1967).

After the initial push by Methodism in St. Augustine, however, the denomination reached a hiatus by 1839 (Brooks, W. E. 1965:9–10). The reasons are not clear, although the overwhelming preponderance of Catholics still in the community may have been the cause. To revive both white and black congregations, the Reverend Simon Peter Richardson arrived in St. Augustine in 1845. That year was a crucial one in the nation, in Florida, and in the Methodist Church. The United States was engaged in the Mexican War, a fact mentioned by Jack in his narrative. More important in the South was the looming threat of secession from the Union by slaveholding states. Significantly, Florida became a state that year and was admitted as a slave state. In that same year, the national Methodist Church split into the northern church and the southern church; divided, as was the nation, into pro- and antislavery factions. A doctrinal crisis arose when the abolitionists—who were Methodists—named slavery a sin and slaveholders, particularly ministers, as sinners. Reverend Richardson, however, was a white secessionist and a member of the newly minted Methodist Episcopal Church South. Thus, his superiors believed him to be an ideal choice for pastor in the town. As matters developed, this proved not to be the case.

The Reverend Richardson found things in disarray when he arrived in St.

Augustine. The church building had been sold and the structure desecrated by use as a workshop and tool shed. Only Jack Smith remained as a loyal Methodist. As the pastor reported it, "On my arrival, no one greeted me, except one negro, named Jack. He thanked the Lord that the missionary had come" (Rivers and Brown 2001:2).

As he remembered the experience almost thirty years later, Richardson found the going rough in St. Augustine. The promised housing fell through, so he needed money to rent lodgings, although local cooperation was totally lacking. He rented a small place in which to preach but could not pay the rent, so he moved to the "Council House," causing a storm of protest in the town. In a letter to the *Southern Christian Advocate*, Richardson complained "the pastor of the Presbyterian Church, who was a Bostonian, did all he could to break me down." Richardson made a last effort to collect money to build a church, "but not a dollar would the dear people give to build a Methodist Church." In despair, Richardson asked, "Has heaven decreed that Methodists shall not dwell in the ancient city?" Thereupon, he retreated back to Charleston (Richardson, S. P. 1874).

A few years after his time in St. Augustine, Richardson showed his proslavery stance in a letter to the *Tallahassee Florida Sentinel*. He was vehement about the need to strike out the "abolitionist" statement in the General Rules forbidding "The buying, and selling, of men, women, and children, with intention to enslave them" (Richardson, S. P. 1850). With slaves as the majority of the St. Augustine congregation, he was not in tune with the black members, thus accounting for his poor showing in the town.

When Richardson failed to revive the Methodist congregation, Jack Smith took on the task of collecting money to build a church, an unusual effort for a black man in the middle of the nineteenth century. He was eminently successful. The old church building was useless—dilapidated in any case—so Jack secured land from Burroughs E. Carr, who, as a good friend of Buckingham Smith, gladly donated the land for the church. Jack found other willing donors among the whites and blacks in town as well as in Savannah. The new church building rose in the shadow of the large Magnolia Hotel on St. George Street, a hotel constructed by Carr in the block north of Treasury Street.

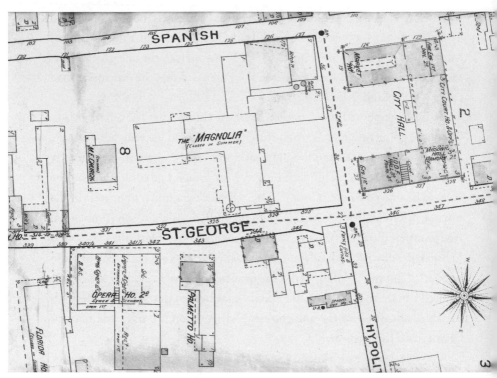

Sanborn Insurance Map of 1893 St. Augustine, showing Uncle Jack's Church
(below #8), labeled on maps at the time as "M.E. Church (Coloured)." Map
Collection, St. Augustine Historical Society. By permission of St. Augustine
Historical Society, St. Augustine, Florida.

Two photographs survive that show part of the new church. The small
rectangular masonry building appears to be in a modified Greek revival style
with characteristic square pillars and a gable-return roofline. The church was
not graced with a bell tower or any other structural adornment, although the
quality of the photographs makes this difficult to determine. Apparently, the
church had two doors in the front as customary separate entrances for men
and women.

For the first time in St. Augustine, a black pastor served black Methodists, and the church was exclusively theirs. Jack tells us that he "exhorted my
brethren from the time of the Mexican War." So, from 1845 almost until
his death, Jack served a black congregation that continued to grow in size.
The meetinghouse, called from that time on "Father Jack's Church" or the

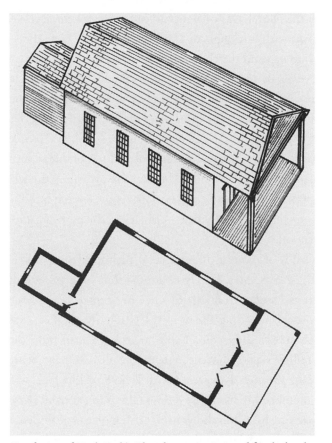

Rendering of Uncle Jack's Church as commissioned for the book.
Fred Amato, 2005. By permission of Fred Amato, St. Augustine, Florida.

"Coloured Methodist Church," was convenient for Jack, located just a short walk from his cabin on the Smith property to the west.

Less than two decades after the church house was built, the Civil War began and the Southern Methodist congregation again fell on difficult political times. For more than a year, southern patriotism flourished in St. Augustine at the same time that the economy collapsed without the annual infusion of northern visitors. On March 11, 1862, matters took a different turn when Union forces captured the town. For the remainder of the war, St. Augustine and northeast Florida were occupied territory, a disorganized situation for all of the southern sympathizers in the community and an increasingly confusing position for the slaves in the town.

Jack Smith's church was without his leadership for three years during the war, as he was with Buckingham Smith in New York, but others soon filled the leadership gap and the church building was used extensively during the Civil War years. By 1863, the National Freedman's Relief Association operated a school in the church building. Four white women from the Northern Methodist Church began the missionary effort. A little later, the American Missionary Association (AMA) sent a couple, Gorham A. Greely and his wife, Harriet, to take charge of the school and to conduct church services. By the end of the war, two hundred blacks were attending the school, as was reported, perhaps with some exaggeration. As the church building had only one room, the pupils were divided—primary in the morning and secondary in the afternoon.

One pupil is of interest. In a letter to Bishop Henry B. Whipple, secretary of the AMA, Mrs. Greely mentions that "one woman over 70 yrs. of age who was stolen from Africa since her remembrance can do better [than the others at reading and writing]"(Richardson, J. M. 1875:182–184; NYFA 1864–1865). This woman appears to have been Judie Smith, Jack's longtime fellow slave, who through the years may have achieved some book learning through association with Jack. She, like Jack, was admitted to church membership by the Reverend Glenn in 1823. An 1875 etching of Jack approaching his cabin shows him leaning on a cane with a woman doing laundry in the background. Although this depiction might indicate a wife, no record of a marriage was found in any documents (Woolson 1875, L(296):169–170).

The American Missionary Association had its headquarters in the church building and visiting preachers occupied the pulpit on Sundays (NYFA 1864–1965; NYAM 1866). This group probably included the Methodist minister who was present when the unofficial Emancipation Proclamation was read in March 1862 in St. Augustine. Mrs. Greely also gave a description of the Sunday services:

These pious people regularly throughout the year, assemble themselves every Sunday morning in the church, before sunrise, for praise and prayer. They are not noisy, as they are in many places, but are quite consistent in their manner of worship. There is a spirituality among them, which like a living flame is constantly burning in their altars, and

Sketch of Uncle Jack's Cabin. *Harper's New Monthly Magazine,*
Harper & Brothers, New York, New York, 1875.

it shows itself in their strong faith, and their sincere and earnest devotion and consistent lives. (NYAM, January 1866)

Her description speaks well of Jack Smith's earlier leadership of his flock.

Jack may have been well aware that his church was being used in a positive
way during his absence. In the years after he returned to St. Augustine, however, matters were somewhat turbulent. C. M. Semple, in a letter of October
1871, reports on a trip to St. Augustine but does not mention Jack, instead
"Mr. Howard our col[ored] minister" is referred to in the letter. According
to the letter, Mr. Howard "and others had dug a trench to drain the lot which
was full of water, cleaned the school house and planted some trees in the
yard." The problems were due to the severe storms with much wind and rain
that St. Augustine had endured in the previous month (Richardson, J. M.
1875:193).

In 1873, after the Civil War, the African Methodist Episcopal (AME) Church was established in St. Augustine, having been originally established in the United States much earlier. Many of the newly freed slaves in St. Augustine, and later their descendants, flocked to worship at a church that was truly their own. Jack did not join this groundswell but remained within the Southern Methodist Episcopal Church. By then, he was in his seventies and established in town, a well-known presence among blacks and whites alike. Furthermore, historian Canter Brown has indicated that the AME Church developed a reputation for activism that may not have been attractive to Jack.[2] Likewise, by that time, he knew that his ordination was under consideration, an honor that credentialed him as a full-fledged Methodist minister in 1868.

Other small black churches in mainline denominations—Baptist, Presbyterian, and Episcopal—began after the Civil War and eventually built their own buildings. Thus, Father Jack's church, as it came to be called, was not the only black congregation with its own church building.

How could Jack have felt standing out among his fellows as a black Methodist leader? Unlike many other locales in the South, black ministers in St. Augustine lived in a special state of grace (see particularly Landers 1988; Marotti 2003). Even after 1845, when repressive state laws for slaves were enacted in Tallahassee, black preachers were accorded special privileges in St. Augustine. For example, they were not subject to the curfew and could move about freely at any time of night. A search of the passes issued by slave masters from 1821 to 1862 did not reveal any pass issued to Jack Smith (COSA, BF 1824–1855). To a certain extent, benign Spanish traditions regarding slaves and freedmen persisted in the town at some level.

Nevertheless, many northerners moving into St. Augustine after 1821 had more ambivalent perceptions of the black population. Even during the time that Jack was preaching, black preachers were not held in high regard in some quarters in St. Augustine. In an article entitled "Negro Preachers" in the local newspaper, a writer notes, "His [referring to black preachers] religion at present, owing to centuries of oppression and darkness is little intellectual but powerfully emotional and sensuous. It sweeps and surges through his whole nature, and utterly controls it" (*St. Augustine Examiner*, May 8, 1867:3).

Even before the Civil War, Jack was not the only black Protestant minister in town. Several other small congregations existed from which black men rose as spiritual leaders among their fellows. We have record of several. Smart Madison has already been mentioned as welcoming the Union forces to St. Augustine in 1862. He was near to Jack in age and began his ministry in the 1820s on the plantation of John Houston McIntosh Madison, which was located near St. Marys, Georgia. "Daddy Smart," as he was called, was the overseer and his wife ran a nursery while the parents of the children worked on the plantation. Smart preached to the other plantation slaves but not always successfully. Some of the other slaves resented him for trying to learn to read; seeing him with a book in hand, they feared that he would get in trouble, be dangerous, and get them accused of plotting a disturbance. Smart thought that they were just "jealous."

By the time of the Civil War, Smart and his wife, too old to work, were under the care of the Dummett family of St. Augustine and were permitted to live in a cabin in town, as Jack was. The congregation that Smart developed in town met in his own small house for Sunday services and Wednesday prayer meetings. As far as is known, this independent congregation dissolved after Smart's death. This pattern may have been common in the town. A black man who felt called to preach the gospel attracted others; then, when the pastor died, his flock dispersed to other congregations. These pastorates were not as substantive or lasting as Jack's, which continued long past his death.

Smart Madison was also not as literate as Jack. Each Saturday, he would need to have a young girl from the Dummett family read him the chapter from the Bible that he planned as the text for his sermon the next morning. The Sunday after the unofficial Emancipation Proclamation was read in March 1862 to the gathered blacks at the Presbyterian Church, he chose John 14 about Jesus promising the Holy Spirit to his disciples at the Last Supper. When the young girl remonstrated with him for not choosing the passage about Moses leading the children of Israel out of Egypt, he insisted on his choice, tartly reminding her that he was the preacher (Cochran 1896:101–136).

Other blacks felt called to preach on special occasions, not always to a regular following but to a collection of family and friends. As an example,

Sippya Tucker applied to the City Commission and received permission to hold a nighttime "prear" meeting on Christmas Eve, 1844. Gatherings of slaves and freedmen at night were generally frowned on, although sometimes a "coloured ball" [dance] was allowed. Exceptions were made for occasions, such as funerals, to take place at night, but even then, a city ordinance required the principals to apply for permission.

Another Protestant black whose status was more like Jack's was Davy Anderson, probably one of the Anderson slaves from the property south of the Smith's. The documents are unclear, however, on the point of whether he was even a slave and, if so, in which Anderson family he was a bondsman. What is clear is the high regard he enjoyed at Holy Trinity Episcopal Church in St. Augustine. While not exactly a minister with credentials, he was definitely the leader and recruiter of blacks to the Episcopal Church, sponsoring thirty-eight blacks for baptism between 1845 and 1856. In largely Catholic St. Augustine, where Protestants had difficulty in proselytizing among blacks, his record almost equaled Jack Smith's. When Davy died in 1856, the remarkable funeral provided for him included two clergymen, one a bishop (Marotti 2003:183–184).

Caleb Simmons appears to have been the ranking black Presbyterian, at least for part of his career. He was also the only black individual mentioned in Jack's narrative. Jack tells us that he and Caleb learned to read the Bible together. Caleb was accepted as a member of the Presbyterian Church in 1827, along with six other black individuals. His wife joined at a later date and their son was baptized in the church. However, by 1833, Caleb had fallen from grace. He was accused of mistreating his wife, as well as other misdeeds, and brought up in front of the elders of the church. Defended by Dr. Andrew Anderson, Caleb admitted his guilt. He was suspended from the church temporarily but later reinstated after he gave public acknowledgement of his faults (Harvey 2005:3–4).

As far as is known, no disgrace ever attached to Jack Smith's ministry. Jack's moral fiber was never questioned, as holding up good behavior as an example to his fellows was part of his ministry. His high standard of conduct assisted him in his role of counselor, advocate, judge, and spiritual leader for the members of his church.

We must assume that Jack Smith was a preacher with a strong element of personal magnetism, but having no record of any of his sermons hampers that assumption. In addition to his record of conversion to Christianity, only one other document found so far provides us with a possible record of Jack's words about his religion. He is mentioned in a letter from Peter Skein Smith to his sister-in-law, Mrs. Garrit (Nancy) Smith, abolitionists both (but not known relatives of the Smiths who owned Jack). When the letter arrived, a number of people were visiting in Peter Skein Smith's home in St. Augustine. He wrote Nancy, ". . . Your servant John and good old father Jack were all [visiting?] when your letter was dropped in. I read parts of it to them, and Old Jack remarked: 'religion is same time *mana*, all over de world, whether pent up in a little cabin at sea: or on shore in a log hut or a manger let but the still small voice of the Holy Spirit whisper to the soul 'Jesus is here'; and the child of God is ready to 'glory in the infinity' which causes his heart to burn within him as he holds sweet communion with . . . .' [the rest of the sentence is unclear]" (PFP June 1835).

While this passage certainly demonstrates Jack's religious "zeal," as described in his obituary, the use of the word "spirit" is of interest in this context. The plural concept of "spirits" is a basic part of West African heritage. Good and bad spirits, as representatives of the dead, are at the core of pagan religions. Even when Muslim or Christian religion is grafted onto a pagan base, the notion of spirits remains as an underlying theme in the African pantheon (Abrahams and Szwed 1983:138–225). The new religion provides the comfort of a traditional understanding in a new wrapper. The use of the expression "Holy Spirit" by Jack and his reference to Jesus, therefore, reflect a deep emotional commitment to Christian belief when used by someone born in Africa. Likewise, *mana* as used by Jack in a religious context means authority, vision, and power received from the supernatural.

Jack's presence at Peter Skein Smith's house gives us pause to consider his association with abolitionists who were either residents in or winter visitors to St. Augustine. The apparent ease of his appearance and comments at the Peter Skein Smith house, as well as the fact that he knew Garrit and Nancy Smith implies an association with prominent members of the northern abolitionist group. Garrit Smith, in particular, spent most of his time working for freedom for the slaves. He was a wealthy man who founded the Liberty Political Party, started his own church based on racial equality, and whose vast estate in New York was a major station on the Underground Railroad through which escaped slaves passed to freedom in Canada. Jack must have heard the arguments for freedom and news of the push toward emancipation from this source. We might assume that he used this information in preaching to his fellow blacks.

Also enlightening is a description by a visitor to St. Augustine of a funeral that Jack conducted in 1852, possibly for another aged slave named Jack. After first describing a Catholic funeral for a child, the author recounts:

> The other [funeral] was that of an old Negro named Jack. The coffin was black and ornamented with brass nails. It was carried on a cart preceded by an old Negro with a long crepe weeper on his hat. The women, neatly dressed, with handkerchiefs on their heads, came immediately after the cart, and then the men followed. There were from sixty to eighty in the procession. Their countenances were grave, and their deportment serious and becoming a solemn occasion. The deceased was a firm member of the Methodist Church and a slave all his life, a man of good conduct and character. (Clinton 1852:21–22)

Jack Smith seems to have been the leader of the procession wearing a "crepe weeper." The question arises as to the identity of this other Jack. A close reading of Clinton's account of life in St. Augustine leads to the tentative conclusion that the documentation may reflect a misunderstanding that the name "Jack" referred not to the corpse but to the well-known black Methodist minister, Jack Smith.

In leading the procession, Jack was following a long-standing African tradition. Funeral processions were an important religious practice for blacks in the Americas. Often to the amazement of the whites, the cortège took the long way to the gravesite, even progressing up and down numerous streets as a last way to honor the deceased and his participation in the community (Abrahams and Szwed 1983:163–179).

Jack's congregation endured through the years. His obituary says that he continued preaching to the last (see Appendix E, "Jack Smith's Obituary"). Yet, the 1880 U.S. Census refers to Jack as a "retired M.E. preacher" (U.S. Census 1880).

The church building was torn down in the early part of the twentieth

Photograph circa 1930s of Trinity United Methodist Church, 82 Bridge Street, St. Augustine, the descendent congregation of Jack Smith's original church. Photographic Collection, St. Augustine Historical Society. By permission of St. Augustine Historical Society, St. Augustine, Florida.

century to make room for a parking lot. Eventually, a new and much larger church was erected on Bridge Street in 1912. Situated on the edge of the Lincolnville area, the traditional African-American section established after the Civil War, Trinity United Methodist Church is the descendant of Father Jack's Church, boasting rightly of being the oldest African-American congregation in St. Augustine.

Religion and his church played an important role in Jack's life as well as in the future life of the town. Religious leadership was something that he developed outside his life as a slave, a way of maximizing things for himself. Also, he fulfilled a role common in West Africa where the religious leader is likewise the civic leader for his group. Not only did he make a contribution to the enrichment of the human spirit, he also fully actualized his own special *mana* within the confines of his slave status. Most important to Jack, he continued as a preacher of the gospel at his church on St. George Street, at least part time, until the day of his death.

Notes

1. Halbirt, personal communication, 2004.
2. Brown, personal communication, 2005.

Jack's Attitude Toward His Enslaved Status

In the early days of slavery, religion was discouraged in the southeastern United States. Even when slaves were allowed to attend services, the parts of the Bible quoted to them by white preachers enforced the idea—at the behest of the owners—that a slave's responsibility was to honor and obey the master. Bound with this constraint, learning to read and write was commonly prevented and often punished, as any learning was believed to send slaves down the path to riot and rebellion. Nevertheless, as the nineteenth century rolled on, religion took a central role—social as well as spiritual—in black cultures in the southern United States. For slaves, religion had special meaning. They gained hope through the belief that Jesus, as champion of the meek and lowly, would set them free. In most instances, the town of St. Augustine was less repressive due to the Spanish Catholic influence, this being particularly true in the early nineteenth century.

What Sitiki thought of his enslaved condition is impossible to understand fully. Nor can we know, except indirectly, what ideas he had about the institution of slavery. Even today, institutions embedded in our culture are taken for granted. In the eighteenth and early nineteenth century in the United States, the institution of slavery was a given, particularly in the South. When Jack was young, he may not have spent many hours contemplating the moral and ethical implications of his status as an enslaved person.

Jack's enslaved condition lasted until emancipation sometime during the Civil War. This involuntary status stretched for seventy or more years of his life. No one reading the narrative can doubt that he was well-treated, even during his youth in Africa. But his situation went beyond receiving the good treatment of others; he carved out a significant position for himself within the Smith family as well as within the St. Augustine community.

Nevertheless, slavery is never good. One ex-slave, Richard Allen, summed it up: "slavery was a bitter pill, notwithstanding we had a good master" (Starling 1988:102).

A more honest view is presented in the narrative of a West African man, Abduhl Rahhahman, later known by the name of James L. Bradley. He told of being taken by the "soul destroyers" at a very young age. In a telling comment, he declared: "How strange it is that anybody should believe that any human body *could* be a slave, and yet be contented! I do not believe there ever was a slave, who did not long for liberty" (Bradley 1828:689).

We can assume that the experiences of slaves are on a continuum from those who were severely treated by their masters, and even died as a result, to those who experienced better treatment even though under, at best, a repressive and dehumanizing system. Jack's story supports the conclusion that he was more fortunate than most in his servitude.

Considering the background and circumstances of Jack Smith's long life, there are some clues as to his attitude toward his enslavement. Starting near the beginning, Sitiki tells of the capture of his family as a traumatic event. Certainly, a capture that early in life sets a pattern of some acceptance of fate as an owned person. Children are accustomed to authority during their early years, whether from parents or others, and, in most cases, do not dwell much on the past or future. Acceptance of the present is foremost.

Sitiki spent his earliest years in a conventional African family. Around their village was a continuous stream of traders and networks that moved the newly enslaved to the coast for transshipment to the Americas. Though he was at first abruptly channeled into this trade stream, Sitiki, unlike many other slaves, spent some years in Africa before he faced the sea voyage.

Initially, the young slave was probably slated to become a victim of the worst of the overseas trade. The one-year interlude on the sheep farm—a time that he tells us little about—must have been a turning point. The focus there, in addition to accustoming the young charges to their life of slavery, was to perform a triage, a winnowing out of the talented from those believed to be more fitted for chattel plantation slavery. Thus, as a boy of promise, Sitiki was sold as a "servant" to an Englishman on the West African coast.

While still in Africa at the coastal trading station, Sitiki experienced a variant of the British slavery system. A domestic slavery system existed in England from early times, largely populated by slaves of white complexion, but such slavery was nearly eradicated by the thirteenth century. Nevertheless, pockets of slavery in the British Isles continued. As late as the seventeenth century, enslavement of the Irish was common. Slavery took its most virulent form, however, after black slaves became available. The British system of African enslavement was characterized by a view of Africans as "the other," assuming a perceived backwardness of their culture, religion, and way of life merely from the color of their skin. Racism, in its worst form, developed. People of color were placed on the lowest rung (barely human) of the rigid British class system. Fortunes were made on the backs of African labor on large-scale British plantations in places such as Jamaica and Barbados. Britain, for a time, had a corner on overseas trade in black human cargo, but this exploitation was eventually decried in some religious and humanitarian enclaves in the homeland, leading to the abolishment of the slave trade in 1807.

The combination of African and British slavery systems under which Sitiki lived in the coastal factory was far different from slavery on a British West Indies plantation. Before he was through with his travels, Sitiki had to learn four types of monetary systems: African shells, British currency, American dollars, and Spanish coinage. In truth, the mixed culture and economic focus in the blend of these systems furnished further informal education for the boy. He began to learn the English language and Anglo-English ways that advanced his prospects. At the same time, he was partially still in the comfort of an African context, particularly since his owner had an African wife. He spoke of being well treated during his time in Africa, and indeed, if his owner, Taylor, had not died, his fate might have been to continue as a slave in Africa.

Instead, when Sitiki was sold as a cabin boy on an American slave ship, he entered a third slavery system, the Anglo-American one. When he reached

Charleston and was later sold in Savannah, he entered the "Old South" slavery system with its extensive and monolithic plantations. The Old South system was one of the most successful in the world, while it lasted, for the planters and slave masters, partly because of the excess of births over deaths in the North Atlantic coastal colonies. This is in comparison, for example, with slavery systems in the West Indies and parts of South America where the demographic picture generally indicated a preponderance of deaths over births in the slave population.

Nevertheless, the colonial slavery system in North America and later the United States system was an offshoot of the repressive British system. In fact, the plantation layout in the South was an adaptation of British plantations in Ireland from the seventeenth century (Brannon 1992). Differences existed, however, between the British and American plantation systems, particularly in the American attempt to increase manpower through births on the plantations.

Thus, a plantation in the American mode was somewhat paternalistic, giving rise to the counterpoint terminology often used at that time by plantation owners of the "white family" and the "slave family." Such terms promoted a false kind of kinship system, far different from the integral one in Africa. These terms reinforced the prevailing white mythology of the "happy slave."

In odd contrast, slavery in the southern states revived the European feudal system yet depended at the same time on the capitalistic economy of industrial Euro-American markets. Sitiki, by then called Jack, worked as an urban slave in Josiah Smith's mercantile establishment, a brokering element between the two sides of the plantation and slave trade duality. Here, perhaps, he began to think of himself as a commodity. In speaking of his status, he commented, "In no instance have I ever known the value given in exchange or the price for which I was sold." If he had attempted to find out, his monetary value would not have been difficult to determine. Many other slaves or ex-slaves were quite specific about the price paid for them. That he was in a certain amount of denial about his slave status is one conclusion that can be drawn.

When Jack moved north to Connecticut with the Smith family, he encountered another variant of the slavery system in the United States, much different from that in the South. As indicated in William Pierson's book, *Black Yankees* (1988), slavery in New England commonly consisted of a few slaves on small farms working alongside the master's family. While there, Jack continued his close association with the Smith family and expanded his associations to include family members who had never left New England. Blacks were still somewhat of a novelty in New England and that fascination helped to bring about the sponsorship of African festivals and celebrations. Several decades after the Smiths moved south again, abolition activities began in earnest in New England. Moral considerations overruled any economic advantages that slavery brought to a region of the country where slavery was limited in practice.

During the time that Jack lived in Connecticut, he was growing out of childhood and able to look at his situation as a slave and as a human being. Right after he described the incident of the dead bird, he affirmed in his narrative, "These circumstances though of no interest to strangers stand out in my lifetime as matters everywhere important to me." Then he concluded, "The vicissitudes and movement of the family everyway concerned my own fortunes." Jack was using the word "fortunes" in its original meaning of accidental or chance occurrences, not in the modern sense to indicate good fortune. He saw that his position as a slave meant that the Smith fortunes became his fortunes, an inescapable fact when he was owned by them for many years and carried their name.

Next, in south Georgia, he was on what appears to have been a small plantation near St. Marys. There, his life was interrupted when he was captured again and offered freedom with no clear view of what it could mean for his future. Was he tempted to leave with the British? Neither his narrative nor other documents reveal his reasons for failing to grasp the opportunity, if indeed it was a real opportunity. Staying with the Smith family had some advantages as, by then, he was entrusted with increased responsibilities and enjoyed more opportunities.

The Smiths' entry into Florida brought Jack into the Spanish slavery system. The Spanish system is generally conceded to have been much more benign than the British or American systems, largely due to the ameliorating influence of the Roman Catholic Church. No matter the color or origin, an individual baptized in the faith was considered fully human in

God's sight, able to partake of all the sacraments, and permitted to marry another Catholic regardless of race. Unlike in the British and American systems, the separation of slaves from family members for sale elsewhere was not an official part of the Spanish system. The Church did not entirely approve of slavery but seems to have considered it a necessary condition (Genovese 1971:63–64).

Unlike the American slavery system and the British system from which it descended, Spanish slaves were not considered chattel and, thus, had access to the court system. The law in Spain was based on ancient Visigothic law and on the Justinian code as adapted into the Spanish system. This hybrid legal code was then further modified in 1680 specifically for the West Indies. The drift of these laws was to ensure justice for those on the lowest rung of society who, regardless of their status, were morally and legally entitled to just treatment. Slaves under Spanish law had the right to acquire and transfer property and to file legal suits in court. Although restricted from certain actions, slaves were, by law, even able to bring suit against their masters for ill treatment. They were also assured of the legal right of *coarctacion*. As this term was defined in the Spanish Americas, *coarctacion* gave the slave a legal right to have a fair price set for his freedom and contract with his owner for that freedom. *Coarctacion* also entailed the owner's legal obligation to accept the purchase terms as set and fulfilled (Landers 1988:11). Nevertheless, abuses occurred, especially in far-flung territories such as Florida, resulting in Spain's enactment of a new slave code in 1789 to ensure humane treatment (Landers 1988:3–6).

When Jack came to St. Augustine at the end of the Second Spanish period, the acquisition of Florida as a territory by the United States was a foregone conclusion. Regardless of the change of flags after 1821, both the U.S. and Spanish legal systems were invoked at different times. For some years after Florida became a U.S. territory, the two systems were even blended in redress of disputes. The benign Spanish influence—at least insofar as slaves were concerned—continued for several decades before Americanization of Florida began in earnest in the 1840s.

St. Augustine at the end of the Spanish hegemony was remarkable for its confusion and polyglot status. One could hear many languages on the streets, particularly on the waterfront: Spanish, Catalan as spoken by the

Minorcans, English, various African dialects, and once in a while French or German. Jack, in his position in the Smith's "store of goods," became acquainted with free blacks as well as slaves and, more remarkable, with members of the black military forces. Some twenty years earlier, in 1796, Jorge Biassou, a leader of the slave rebellion in Haiti, along with some of his followers moved to St. Augustine, where he served as a role model of achievement and independence for local blacks—but also of arrogance. The Spanish authorities used the military skills of Biassou and his men in the early nineteenth century, especially in tracking down hostile Indians who were increasingly active after 1803. Although General Biassou died before Jack entered town in 1817, some of Biassou's retinue including their families still remained. Jack was no doubt aware that this group practiced Catholicism and sometimes pagan religion as well (Landers 1988:85–100).

The description of St. Augustine in Chapter 10 is presented as Jack's memory of the Spanish town when he arrived, whereas he actually wandered beyond that time in his recollections with Buckingham. As noted, he described Fort Mose, several miles north of Castillo San Marco, as a refuge for slaves escaping from other southern states during the First Spanish period. Jack mentions these freedmen without a trace of envy in the telling, his tone being more of interest.

Another freed group came to town in October 1828. These 111 Africans, all men, were part of the cargo of the slave ship, *Guerrero*, wrecked off the Florida Keys. U.S. Marshal Waters Smith escorted them to St. Augustine with the intention of repatriating them to Africa. Many months passed before arrangements for transshipment to Africa could be made through the American Colonization Society. In the meantime, they were farmed out to several plantations—mostly the Zephaniah Kingsley and Joseph Hernandez plantations—to keep them occupied and to have them earn their keep during the interim. On August 21, 1829, those who had not died, escaped, or been hidden by their temporary masters, left for Liberia. There, they suffered some initial hardships before finally settling in a location that became known as New Georgia (Swanson 2005:57–82). How many of these Africans were temporarily housed close to St. Augustine or how many remained in Florida is not known. However, Jack could not help but be aware of them, though most were Congo or Eboe people from locations farther south than

Jack's original home in West Africa, and thus spoke different languages from his own native tongue.

The story of Governor Jose Coppinger's two "servants" (actually slaves) is instructive of the complex dynamics that could exist between slaves and their masters. Coppinger bargained with his slaves, offering freedom once their price was worked out. Yet, when their freedom was finally earned, they wanted to stay on in the governor's employ. Coppinger refused, saying, according to Jack's memory, "nature was best served where gratitude and honor are not permitted to wander far from what may be necessity."

Jack's mention in his narrative of the hymn, "When I Can Read my Title Clear," is illustrative. This hymn was written by Isaac Watts, a nonconformist in religion, and set to music by William Mather. Although sung by both white and black congregations in the early nineteenth century, the hymn had special meaning for slaves. The word "title" refers to the slave's last name, which was commonly the master's name (Abrahams and Szwed 1983:356–369). As slaves, they had no choice about that, but the first name was usually thought of as one's own. Sometimes, with several owners in a lifetime, slaves did not clearly understand that they had a last name, even if temporary. They might have heard themselves referred to as "Mr. Wilson's Lucy," for example, and not as "Lucy Wilson." After emancipation, part of freedom was assuming the responsibility and privilege of establishing original last names. Thus, a clear title was a mark of freedom (Abrahams and Szwed 1983:360–362). The words of the first stanza of this well-known hymn are:

> When I can read my title clear to mansions in the skies
> I bid farewell to every fear, and wipe my weeping eyes
> There shall I bathe my weary soul in seas of heavenly rest
> And not a wave of trouble roll across my peaceful breast.
> (Housewright 1991:317–318)

Buckingham Smith, who was very young at the time but able to read, used the song in order to help Jack learn to read.

According to Bruce Gardow, a United Methodist Church minister in Wisconsin, the hymn symbolically embodies the two kinds of freedom acknowledged in Protestant theology: freedom in the secular and legal sense, as well as freedom in the spiritual sense. The strong belief existed among slaves—particularly in the nineteenth century—that Jesus would in time set them free. The song was taught to the *Amistad* slaves during their sojourn in New England as they awaited shipment back to Africa. The hymn, then, is a message about the agony experienced in this world and the ultimate joy to be experienced in heaven.[1]

Jack rarely used the word "slave" in his narrative, preferring the words "servant," "black," or in one instance, "coloured." Again, these usages may have been euphemisms congenial for his white former master in the postslavery times when the narrative was written down. As the narrative progressed and Jack described his life in St. Augustine, he increasingly used the first-person plurals "we" and "us," perhaps identifying himself by then as part of the extended household of the Smiths.

Besides Judie, Jack's fellow slave in the Smith household, only one other black person is mentioned in the narrative: Caleb, with whom Jack learned to read the Bible. The omission of other names may indicate that he was somewhat of a loner, especially since he became, as he grew older, one of the last African-born blacks in St. Augustine. In fact, the beginning of his narrative addresses "sons of Africans." His ascendance as a Methodist minister in a prominent black congregation—and, thus, a leader of his people—put him in an insulated position, although many black acquaintances were a likely part of his life. Given the size of the town, he must have known every black or white person in the community by sight

In that leadership position, Jack, or at least Jack's Methodist Church, may have played a part in quelling a suspected slave insurrection. In a documented case, Emanuel Aquair reported that, on the night of May 1, 1837, he heard some "negroes" conversing in the street, one being Jim, formerly a slave of George Gibbs, but by then a slave of a black freedman, and presently a member of Jack's church. On that occasion, he heard Jim say, ". . . let them go on—let them frolic—our time will come." Aquair believed that "the Negroes were preparing to rise." The next morning, he heard one of the same men say, "Now is the time as soon as the steamboat goes." He was then even more convinced that the blacks were "preparing to do some offensive acts against the white population of the city."

Francis W. Andrew was also concerned. He had seen "a number of Negroes with large sticks or clubs in their hands," hanging about between Manucy's corner and Solana's corner. Emanuel Garrido, another white man, agreed that he had seen something similar, but he vouched for Jim, since he had heard "nothing unfavorable of him, he always conducted himself respectfully." Jim, the suspected ringleader, and Betsy, a slave of Jose Simian Sanchez, both gave depositions. Betsy insisted that Jim was talking to the group about "religious matters and the gospel," both Betsy and Jim being members of the Methodist Church. Jim denied any knowledge of talk, of frolic, of the steamboat, or of the harbor and proceeded to describe his activities in great detail, mundane as they were. He also mentioned that, in addition to religious matters, they were talking about Jim's wife, Venus, who did not treat Betsy well. Venus was "once a member of the Church, but has not lately acted up to her profession." Jim asked why Betsy had not "let him know before so that he might complain to the Church [i.e., Jack Smith as minister] and have things settled" (COSA, BF 1837).

The inquiry seems to have been dropped because of the respect accorded to Jack's church and his congregation and, perhaps, because of Jim's good reputation. In retrospect, the white "frolic" that was alluded to was probably a May Day celebration, a part of festival life for Anglo-Americans at the time. The steamboat added festivity to the occasion, as steam was just then beginning to replace sail, and a steamboat arriving in the harbor was of major interest. The talk of the black inhabitants may have been simply the grumbling of those not in on the party. Jim might have been reassuring them that in heaven things would be different for them. Alternatively, his comment might have actually represented the seed of serious unrest. In retrospect, more than a century and a half later, no firm conclusion is possible, but the incident is evidence of the respect accorded Jack's church.

The lot of a freedman was a problematic position. Attitudes toward blacks altered after the teachings of abolition in the northern United States were perceived as a threat in the southern states and particularly after the 1831 Nat Turner rebellion in Virginia and other similar uprisings. Against this national backdrop, the state of Florida enacted repressive laws discouraging manumission (legal freedom). Hostility and suspicion toward the black populace became an accepted white attitude.

Even in St. Augustine, free blacks were suspect, and each free black needed a patron to vouch for him or her. As Americanization took place and statehood loomed, more repressive laws were passed. When Florida achieved statehood in 1845, rigidity in the two-caste racial system in St. Augustine increased. After that time, manumissions decreased to a trickle. In some years, this town that once contained an unusual number of free blacks, recorded no manumissions at all (Marotti 2003:129–131).

As an example of the repression of blacks in St. Augustine in the years before the Civil War, the City Council published and posted in the market the following ordinance:

> Be it hereby Ordained by the Mayor and Alderman of the City of St. Augustine in Council convened that it shall be and is made the duty of the City Marshall to Ring at 9 Oclock [*sic*] each night the Bell lately placed on the Beef Market as a warning to the Negroes in the City to retire to their respective homes or usual places of Sleeping—and any negro or mulatto caught in the Street or away from his said usual place of sleeping more than thirty minutes after said ringing of the Bell, (without a written pass from the owner or person having the legitimate management or control of such Negro or mulatto for the time being authorizing him to be so away from his said usual place of sleeping) Shall on conviction, be fined in the sum of Two Dollars or punished by the infliction on the bare back of said Negro of not less than Twenty nor more than Thirty Stripes . . . ." (COSA, CCM, Ordinance Number One 1853)

The taint of slavery lingered even after the slaves were free. In the 1864 Census in St. Augustine, Jack Smith is listed as seventy-five years old and as "formerly a slave" (U.S. DOA, SC 1864). Likewise, in his will, Buckingham fixed Jack in status when he referred to him as "once my slave." Seemingly, Buckingham was less concerned about slavery than about uniting the fractured nation, an opinion held also, at least initially, by Abraham Lincoln.

One historian (Marotti 2003:183–186) referred to Jack as "quasi-free." As with several other men in St. Augustine, his status was somewhere between slave and free, in part because of the respected position that Buckingham Smith enjoyed in the town and also because of Jack Smith's own respected position as a preacher. This favored status was strictly informal, not legal. He was still by law a slave.

We may wonder what Buckingham's attitude toward slavery was. These few words of his are only a metaphor and, in any case, come to us second-hand. A.J. Wall, president of the New York Historical Society, quoted Buckingham in a speech given at the unveiling of a marker dedicated to him in St. Augustine. Referring to how he was treated by the ambassador in Spain, Buckingham is reported to have said, "I have been cussed & charged with all sorts of dirty acts, and I have been watched as an overseer looks after a vicious slave" (Wall 1941:18).

However, near the end of his narrative, Jack mentioned that men had changed in their way of thought and that he himself had changed. Such a comment may have been a veiled way for him to show that his attitude toward slavery changed and, since becoming a freedman, was still changing. The slave/master dynamic, like any other relationship, evolves through time. The maturation of individuals, changes in circumstance, the press of other relationships, psychological and physical accompaniments of aging, and the ever-evolving cultural surroundings necessarily compel continual reevaluation of the involuntary alliance.

How might Jack have thought that he had changed? In his narrative, he is modest, remarking that his knowledge is limited to "intercourse with men and what my experience teaches." He seemed to be almost in a poetic and nostalgic vein as he said, "the labors of my mature life have been confined to this field and these trees." Drawing on markers in his own life, he then described learning to read, his ministry, and changes in the landscape around his cabin. The last sentence tails off in describing the "mulberries about the dwelling doubtless from the forest, certainly attained great dimensions were originally nine, of which two have been destroyed by . . . ."

Jack Smith died at 4:00 a.m. on Sunday morning, September 3, 1882. His obituary in the St. Augustine paper was headed "Old Father Jack Dead" and went on to explain, "He was as well as common last evening and old age and chronic complaint bore him off in the ripe time of probably 105 years." More than three hundred people, both black and white, attended the funeral at the church. His body was borne to the grave "in a neat wooden coffin with neat ornaments and plated handles . . . ." The writer of the obituary believed that "tens of thousands of people all over the North will be pained to hear of 'Father Jack's' death.'" The glowing account concluded, "At sunset was laid to

Stereoscopic image circa 1870–1882 of Uncle Jack in his last years in front of his cabin.
Robert N. Dennis Collection of Stereoscopic Views of African Americans in Florida,
Schomburg Center for Research in Black Culture, New York Public Library.
By permission of the New York Public Library, New York, New York.

rest the ashes of a man whose skin was black, but whose hopes were as bright
as those of any mortal that ever lived or died." On his coffin, as a last touch,
"was placed some cuttings from a date palm, which he planted years upon
years ago."

Note

1. Gardow, personal communication, 2005.

Epilogue

Jack Smith and Judie Smith died within two years of each other. The burial permit (death certificate) for Jack Smith reads, "This certifies that I attended Rev. J. Smith and that he died of old age September 3rd 1882 aged 95." The "9" has an extra line through it and the "5" is very lightly written, as though a question remains about the recorded age (COSA, BP #65, folder 5). Dewitt Webb, M.D., signed the death certificate.

The burial permit for Judie Smith reads that she died at the "ME Colored home of asthenia" on October 31, 1880. Asthenia is described as debility or diminution of vital forces; in other words, old age. No age at death is given. Dr. Andrew Anderson signed the death certificate (COSA, BP #65, folder 3).

With some certainty, we can say that both Judie and Jack were buried in the "Huguenot Cemetery" north of the city gate, probably in the unmarked graves on the north side. This cemetery was the only one in use by city Protestants for some years. Buckingham Smith and his wife, as well as his mother, are buried in the white section.

The two-story "Colored Home," built by the Buckingham Smith Benevolent Association on the west bank of the Maria Sanchez Creek, was closed in 1883. The stated reason was that blacks did not like to live in multistory structures. The building then underwent a number of changes, first becoming a school for black boys before being sold and converted into the Buckingham Hotel catering to white tourists. The Benevolent Association, however, continued its care of elderly and infirm blacks in various facilities through the years. The association's funds are presently allotted to the large, modern Bayview Care Center and Pavilion (now racially integrated) in south St. Augustine and to the Buckingham-Smith Assisted Living Facility. This legacy, of sorts, reflects the continuing influence of Buckingham Smith and his former slave, Jack Smith.

Appendix A. Chronology

1794–1796   Approximate birth of Sitiki.

1798–1801   Capture of Sitiki at four- or five-years-old by slave raiders.

1800–1801   Sitiki on sheep farm for one year under African slave system.

1801–1807   Sitiki as house slave to proprietors of two British slave factories (Taylor and the other unknown).

1807   Middle Passage.

————   Sitiki arrives in Charleston, South Carolina, on the brig *Sally*.

1808   Sitiki arrives in Savannah, Georgia, on the brig *Sally* in February.

————   Sitiki, renamed Jack, is sold to Josiah Smith in Savannah in March.

————   Jack moves to Watertown, Connecticut, with the Smiths.

1809   Josiah Smith moves family and slaves to St. Marys, Georgia.

1810   Buckingham Smith born in Cumberland Island, Georgia.

1815   Anita Smith, Buckingham's sister, born in Fernandina, Florida.

————   Jack and other slaves captured in south Georgia by British Admiral George Cockburn.

————   Jack turns down opportunity for freedom offered by Admiral Cockburn.

1817   Jack sails Smith family schooner into harbor of St. Augustine, East Florida, in May.

1823   Death of Josiah, Buckingham Smith's older brother.

———   Buckingham Smith and his sister Anita are confirmed as members of Trinity Episcopal Church.

———   Jack joins the Methodist Church and is baptized on a Sunday in December.

———   Judie Smith, Jack's longtime fellow slave, joins the Methodist Church.

1824   Buckingham Smith goes to Mexico to join his father who was with the U.S. Legation to Mexico.

1825   Death of Josiah Smith.

1826   Jack's ownership transferred to Hannah Smith, Josiah's widow.

1836   Buckingham Smith earns law degree from Harvard.

1837   ———joins law office in Portland, Maine, and becomes Justice of the Peace.

1839   ———returns to Florida and establishes a law practice.

1840s   ———is Secretary to Territorial Governor in St. Augustine, the capital.

1843   ———marries Julia Gardner of Concord, New Hampshire.

———   ———purchases twenty-two acres in St. Augustine and builds a home for his new wife.

1845   Jack raises money to build small Methodist church, known informally as "Father Jack's Church."

———   ———begins to preach at the church, though not officially yet a minister.

1850   Death of Anita Smith Porter, Buckingham's sister.

———   Buckingham Smith is appointed secretary to the U.S. legation to Mexico.

1852   ———Buckingham and his wife return to St. Augustine from Mexico.

1856   ———Buckingham appointed to U.S. legation to Spain.

1858   Death of Hannah Smith, Buckingham's mother.

———   Buckingham Smith returns to St. Augustine from Spain to settle the family estate.

1859   Buckingham takes over ownership of the twelve Smith family slaves upon probate of his mother's estate.

1861   Death of Julia Smith, Buckingham's wife.

1862   Confederate government of Florida attempts to confiscate Buckingham Smith's property.

——   Jack and Buckingham Smith go to New York for the duration of the Civil War.

1864   Union census in St. Augustine lists Jack Smith as seventy-five years old and "formerly a slave."

——   Buckingham returns briefly to St. Augustine, leaving Jack in New York.

——   Buckingham is Florida delegate to National Republican Convention in Baltimore.

——   Buckingham Smith's book on the explorations of Giovanni da Verrazanno is published.

1865   Buckingham's most significant book, *Narratives of Hernando de Soto*, is published.

1868   Jack is credentialed as a full-fledged Methodist minister.

1869   Buckingham and Jack collaborate on "The Story of Uncle Jack."

1871   Buckingham dies in New York as a result of apoplexy and heart problems.

1875   Article about Jack published in *Harpers New Monthly Magazine* with etching of him at his cabin.

1880   U.S. census lists Jack as ninety, a "retired M.E. preacher" born in Africa.

1882   Death of Jack Smith on Sunday morning, September 3.

Appendix B. Condition of the Manuscript

Written and sent to the New York Historical Society Library
subsequent to 1988 trip to the facility.

The Story of Uncle Jack. Probable date of the manuscript, 1868–1869.

Condition of the manuscript in the Buckingham Smith Collection, New
York Historical Society, #2814 on page 457 of *Guide to the Manuscript Collection*.

There appear to be two drafts of the manuscript, although determining
which was written first is difficult. For convenience, I will label them draft
one and draft two.

Draft one is on lined paper with corrections both in ink and pencil, which
would indicate that the corrections may have been done at different times.
There are many scratchovers. Some whole pages appear to have been struck
over as though they were to be discarded. Elsewhere, parts of pages are pasted
over. The pagination of this draft is unclear. On the back of the last page is
written "Sitiki," which was the African name of "Uncle Jack." Several small
scraps with partial sentences written on them, which were found in another
box, seem to be part of this draft.

Draft two is mostly written on half pages of blue paper. There are subtitles,
but the sequence is unclear. As in draft one, the pagination is unclear, and
there are many strikeovers and changes as well as some repetitions. This draft

was packaged in brown wrapping paper that is falling apart but on which can be read "Manuscript of the Story of Uncle Jack (Sitiki) and what appears to be a history of St. Augustine as given by Uncle Jack—First Drafts and copies." This notation is not in Buckingham Smith's handwriting. The assumption is that this was written by the person who went through Buckingham Smith's papers after his death.

A possible beginning of another draft on white paper was found, which has better structure and ends about one third through the manuscript. Also found was a page of random notes on the back of a letter with a notation at the bottom: "for profitable reflexion [*sic*]."

Without doubt the manuscript was still a work in progress at the time of Buckingham Smith's death in 1871.

Patricia C. Griffin
July 1988

Appendix C. Analysis of Sitiki's Language

From: "James Essegbey" <essegbey@aall.ufl.edu>
To: "Valentin Vydrine" <vydrine@VV1964.spb.edu>
CC: "Thomas Bearth <Thomas_Bearth@compuserve.com>; Patricia
C. Griffin <pgriffin@aug.com>
Sent: Friday, April 29, 2005 9:22 AM
Subject: RE: Pastor's Language

Dear Valentin,
I hope you are doing well. Thank you very much for your detailed comments. This is very intriguing indeed! I am sure Patricia will have some further questions. I am therefore sending this mail to you all so she can pick up the communication from there. My many thanks to Prof. Bearth for forwarding the words to you.

Patricia, what do you think?

Best wishes,
James

Valentin Vydrine wrote:

Dear James,

Thomas Bearth passed me you[r] letter concerning Patricia Griffin's questions. Here is what I can say.

The language in question belongs most probably to the Manding group or to the Mokole (Mogofin—Kakabe—Koranko—Lele) group, which is very close to Manding: 11 terms out of 13 belong to the common Manding-Mokole stock (exceptions: #1 bande, #13 coro, #6 is doubtful, I guess, it may be word "sene" for "field, farm").

The vocalism is close to the West Manding variants (such as Mandinka, Xasonka, or Jaxanka): if we consider the transcription of vowels as reflecting the pronunciation, "bulu," "musu" are exactly the forms that we have in those variants (in Bamana or Maninka, we would rather have "bulo" and "muso," in Maninka of Guinea, "bolo" and "moso").

On the other hand, the nouns in the list do not have a definite article -o that is typical of all the West Manding languages.

There are some forms that testify for the closeness of this language to the Mokole group. So, the form "ninki" for "cow" (cf. Koranko: ninki, Kakabe: ningi). #1 "bande" may be compared with a word for "day" in Kakabe: "banda."

The counter-evidence is that all Mokole languages have a definite article -i or -e, and nouns in isolation should normally have it.

The form "sebo" for "meat" is also strange: in Maninka, we have "sobo"; in Bamana, "sogo"; in Mokole Languages, it has a -g- inside, rather than -b-. On the other hand, a form with -b- is typical of Soso (which lies outside the Manding group). A form "sibe/sibo" is attested in Jeri, a small dispersed language in the NE Cote d'Ivoire; but it is too far away and too insignificant from sociolinguistic viewpoint.

The word 9. "ass" = "shofala," tends toward forms of the Mande languages of Sierra Leone, Liberia, and Cote d'Ivoire. By origin, it is a combination of "so," "horse," and "fali," "donkey"; in Maninka and Bamana "sofali" means "mule."

The final diagnosis is: if we consider those forms as correctly transcribed, this language cannot be identified with any modern language. It has some similarities with West Manding languages, some similarities with Mokole languages (especially Koranko and Kakabe), but cannot be recognized as any of them. It is probable that it was one of smaller Futa Jallon Mande languages of the Mokole group that disappeared under the pressure of the theocratic power of Fulbe. We should also keep in mind that the linguistic geography of Futa Jallon is still understudied; during my short trip to the Kakabe area in 2001, I learned about so-called "kuru-Maninka" (or "Mountain Maninka") living around Poredaka, and also about some other smaller isolated populations speaking their particular languages (presumably belonging to the Mande family) which are totally unknown to the scholars.

It's what I can say about this matter.

Valentin Vydrine <vydrine@VV1964.spb.edu>

Museum of Anthropology

University of St. Petersburg, Russia

Friday, 29 April 2005 14:29 +0300 MSK

1. fire = bande

2. water = gui

3. hand = bulu

4. woman = musu

5. knife = muru

6. corn/maise = seno

7. meat = sebo

8. horse = sho

9. ass = shofala

10. cow = sigui or ninki

11. fowl = sese

12. dog = wulu

13. rice = coro

Appendix D. Buckingham Smith's
Last Will and Testament

I Buckingham Smith of St. Augustine do[?] make this my last will and Testament hereby revoking all wills heretofore by me made.

To the Negro Jack—once my slave—I give and devise for his use as long as he shall live the land in St. Augustine belonging to me on both sides of the Maria Sanchez Creek each of the orange grove of my homestead and during his natural life the use of the house he now occupies & the ground in his possession of which it stands together with the products of the trees thereon. Said ground bounded on the north by land belonging to the W[unclear] on the east by the same orange hedge included thereon on the South by a pecan tree also included and met by a fence the whole measuring about 42 yards on each side.

Of my oil paintings, I give to Rebecca Peck representing Morning and Evening by Bergham—to George Riggs of Washington a head by Rebera—to Maria J.B. Browne a cottage scene by Gainesboro—to the Catholic Church a little Spanish picture the Ascension of St. Francis.

To Sallie the elder daughter of John Earl & Eunice Williams I give of my personal property a string of pearls—to their younger daughter I give a silver tray having handles (one of a pair) and to Frances B. Porter my nephew the other silver tray together with all the plate—marked H.G & J.H.S. the silver dishes and milk cup—

My manuscripts of historical character I give to the New York Historical Society with the reservation that during the lifetime of John Gilvary Shea they be for his consultation and use & and [sic] none other & and [sic] for such use may be drawn from the custody of the Society any of them.

To Maria J. Clarke of Hartford Conn. I give $500 interest thereon from my death bill [expense?] bill payment—to my cousin Mrs. Hewell I give my watch—to her daughter the gold necklace—to the daughter of my Curtess [?] the cross of St. Iago.

To Uncle Jack my personal apparel—to Juda, Bunah and Tina—once my servants each one hundred dollars.

The rest of my property real personal and mixed of which I [be] possessed I give and bequeath to Maria J. B. Browne of Springfield Mass. For the use of the black people of St. Augustine and their successors in all time to come on such manner as she shall chose [sic] to adopt by sale devise purchase investment as well endowment—or other ways as well as the interest & issues therefrom providing first for the aged and invalid of those blacks which have been mine. & should she not be in life I give and bequest the same in trust with equal power and instruction to Dr. Oliver Bronson of Florida & for the execution of this my will. I make constitute Maria J. B. Browne to be the sole executrix & should she at any time fail as such—then in her stead I appoint Dr. Oliver Bronson & neither of them shall give bond for the faithful performance of their trusts nor shall the manner in which they shall dispose of or invest my property or discharge them be questioned or either of them be made answerable to any person or persons thereon or before any tribunal.

And I charge my Executor to attend to and relieve the wants of those Negroes who have belonged to me also the children of those who may need and are not undeserving by their conduct of assistance support and protection.

Should a tomb stone not already have been placed over the remains of my wife I direct that $1000 be employed in erecting a monument to mark her grave.

In witness whereof I have herewith set my hand & seal this 17th day April this year 1869.

(signed) Buckingham Smith

Witnesses: Matthew Salano

Louis M Coxetter

W. Howell Robinson

Signed 15 July 1869

Appendix E. Jack Smith's Obituary

Old Father Jack Is Dead

[Newspaper clipping, no date, Ammidown Scrapbook, St. Augustine Historical Society Collections. Actual date of death—September 3, 1882. Videx may have been the pseudonym for Holmes Ammidown, a frequent winter visitor to St. Augustine.]

Old Father Jack is gone! He passed away this morning at 4 o'clock. He was as well as common last evening and old age and chronic complaint bore him off in the ripe time of probably 105 years.

His history is bound up with that of St. Augustine, Fla. He was a native of Africa, brought to America when perhaps 13 years old, and at the time of his death weighed 135 pounds, and was about five feet high. He was imported by the captain of a trading vessel, and was sold to the late Buckingham Smith's father before the latter was born. He lived in Savannah, Charleston, Fernandina and St. Augustine. He was taken prisoner during the War of 1812, but upon the plea of his master he was released. He was a very devout man, and for upward of fifty years he was a minister of the gospel of the Methodist Episcopal Church. He was known far and near, and tens of thousands of people all over the north will be pained to hear of "Father Jack's" death. His burning zeal knew no rank, but to high and low he spoke the glowing

words of love and life. His influence was exerted and successfully in collecting means to build an excellent house of worship on St. George street, and it
was ever known as "Father Jack's church." Collections were sent from Savannah and many other places.

At church this 5 p.m., his body was borne in a neat wooden coffin with
neat ornaments and plated handles, and on it was placed some cuttings from
a date palm which he planted years upon years ago. Over three hundred
friends gathered to hear the simple and heartfelt expressions for his memory and honor. The long procession that followed his remains showed how
greatly respected he was by the city. At sunset was laid to rest the ashes of a
man whose skin was black, but whose hopes were as bright as those of any
mortal that ever lived or died. "His life in its beauty and its duty, was one of
lofty purpose and sincere reality." Videx

Bibliography

Abrahams, Roger D., and John F. Szwed, eds. 1983. *After Africa*. New Haven: Yale University Press.

Anderson, Andrew. 1923. Letter to Robert Ransom. Anderson-Gibbs Collection, St. Augustine Historical Society.

Anonymous. 1819. *Narrative of a Voyage to the Spanish Main, in the Ship "Two Friends."* Facsimile reproduction, 1978. Gainesville: University Press of Florida.

Anonymous. October 30, 1862. "Emancipation in St. Augustine." *Circular Letter* 11:4. Oneida, New York. (Originally published in *Independent Democrat*, New Hampshire.)

Bemrose, John. 1966. *Reminiscences of the Second Seminole War*, edited by John K. Mahon. Gainesville: University Press of Florida.

Bergman, Peter M. 1969. *The Chronological History of the Negro in America*. New York: Harper and Row.

Berlin, Ira. 1980. "Time, Space, and the Evolution of Afro-American society." *American Historical Review* 1:44–78.

Bidwell, Percy. 1916. "Rural Economy in New England at the Beginning of the Nineteenth Century." *Transactions of the Connecticut Academy of Arts and Sciences* 20:241–399.

Bohannon, Paul. 1964. *Africa and Africans*. Garden City, N.Y.: Natural History Press.

Bradley, James L. (Abduhl Rahhahman). 1828. In *Slave Testimony: Two Centuries of Letters, Speeches, Interviews, and Autobiographies*, edited by John Blasssingame, 1977:686–690. Baton Rouge: Louisiana State University.

Brannon, Nick. 1992. "Archaeology of the 17th Century Plantation in Ulster." Paper presented at the 25th annual meeting of the Society for Historical Archaeology, Kingston, Jamaica.

Brooks, George E. 1998. "Climate and History in West Africa." In *Transformations in*

Africa: Essays on Africa's Later Past, edited by Graham Connah, 139–159. London and Washington: Leicester University Press.

Brooks, William E. 1965. *History Highlights of Florida Methodism.* Fort Lauderdale, Fla. Tropical Press.

Bullard, Mary E. 1983. *Black Liberation on Cumberland Island in 1815.* DeLeon Springs, Fla.: E. O. Painter Printing.

Bushnell, Amy Turner. 1981. *The King's Coffer, Proprietors of the Spanish Florida Treasury: 1565–1702.* Gainesville: University Press of Florida.

———. 1994. *Situado and Sabana: Spain's Support System for the Presidio and Mission Provinces of Florida.* Anthropological Papers of the American Museum of Natural History 74.

Cathedral Parish Records (CPR). 1784–1809. White Deaths, vol. 1. Cathedral Basilica of St. Augustine, Florida.

Chapelle, Howard I. 1965. *The History of American Sailing Ships.* New York: W. W. Norton.

Charleston, South Carolina, County of. 1810. Property Information System 457-16-04-024.

Clark, George L. 1914. *A History of Connecticut: Its People and Institutions.* 2nd edition, n.d. New York: G. P. Putnam's Sons.

Clinton, C. A. 1852. *A Winter From Home.* New York: J. F. Trow Printer.

Cochran, M. A. 1896. *Posie or From Reveille to Retreat.* Cincinnati, Ohio: Robert Clarke Company.

Columbian Museum and Savannah Advertizer (CMSA). 1806–1807. Savannah: Georgia Historical Society.

Conneau, Theophilus. 1976. *A Slaver's Log Book: Or 20 Years' Residence in Africa.* New York: Avon Books, reprinted from original 1853 manuscript.

Curtin, Philip D. *The Images of Africa: British Ideas and Action, 1780–1850.* Madison: University of Wisconsin Press.

Cusick, James G. 1993. "Ethnic Groups and Class in an Emerging Market Economy: Spaniards and Minorcans in Late Colonial St. Augustine." PhD diss., University of Florida.

———. 2003. *The Other War of 1812: The Patriot War and the American Invasion of Spanish Florida.* Gainesville: University Press of Florida.

DeCorse, Christopher R. 1998. "The Europeans in West Africa: Culture Contact, Continuity and Change." In *Transformations in Africa: Essays on Africa's Later Past,* edited by Graham Connah. London: Leicester University Press.

Dewhurst, William W. 1881. *The History of St. Augustine.* New York: G. P. Putnam's Sons.

Donnan, Elizabeth. 1935. "The Border Colonies and the Southern Colonies." In *Documents Illustrative of the Slave Trade,* vol. IV. Washington, D.C.: Carnegie Institution.

East Florida Papers (EFP). 1785–1823. Records of Criminal Proceedings. Microfilm. St. Augustine Historical Society.

Emerson, Ralph Waldo. 1827. "Little Journal at St. Augustine." Cabot's Q. R. U. Ralph Waldo Emerson Collections. Cambridge: Houghton Library, Harvard University.

Fage, J. D. 1991. "Hawkins' Hoax? A Sequel to Drake's Fake." *History in Africa* 18:83–91.

Foster, George M. 1960. *Culture and Conquest: America's Spanish Heritage.* New York: Viking Fund Publications in Anthropology 27.

Gannon, Michael V. 1965. *The Cross in the Sand: The Early Catholic Church in Florida, 1813–1870.* Gainesville: University Press of Florida.

Genovese, Eugene D. 1971. *The World the Slaveholders Made.* New York: Vintage Books.

Gibbs, James L., Jr. 1965. *Peoples of Africa.* New York: Holt, Rinehart and Winston.

Glasse, Cyril. 1989. *The Concise Encyclopedia of Islam.* New York: Harper and Row.

Glenn, Joshua Nichols. 1945. "A Diary of Joshua Nichols Glenn." *Florida Historical Quarterly* 24:121–161.

Glicksberg, Charles I. 1936. "Letters of William Cullen Bryant from Florida." *The Florida Historical Quarterly* 14(4):255–274.

Gooch, Anthony, and Angel Garcia de Paredes. 1978. *Cassell's Spanish-English, English-Spanish Dictionary.* New York: Macmillan.

Gordon, Elsbeth K. 2002. *Florida's Colonial Architectural Heritage.* Gainesville: University Press of Florida.

Graham, Thomas. 1978. *The Awakening of St. Augustine.* St. Augustine, Fla.: The St. Augustine Historical Society.

———. 1986. "The Home Front: Civil War Times in St. Augustine." *El Escribano* 23:19–46. St. Augustine Historical Society.

———, ed. 1996. "St. Augustine, 1867: Drawings by Henry J. Morton." *El Escribano* 33. St. Augustine Historical Society.

Greene, Lorenzo Johnston. 1969. *The Negro in Colonial New England.* New York: Atheneum. (Originally published 1942, New York: Columbia University Press.)

Griffin, Patricia C. 1988. "Condition of the manuscript in the Buckingham Smith Collection." *Guide to the Manuscript Collection* 2814:457. New York Historical Society.

———. 1991. *Mullet on the Beach: The Minorcans of Florida, 1768–1788.* Gainesville: University Press of Florida.

———. 1995. "Ralph Waldo Emerson in St. Augustine." Monograph reprinted from *El Escribano* 32:113–134. St. Augustine Historical Society.

———. 1999. "The Halifax-Misquitoes Plantation Corridor: An Overview." *The Florida Anthropologist* 52(1–2):5–23.

———, and Diana Edwards. 1990. "Richard Aloysius Twine: Photographer of Lincolnville (1922–1927)." Unpublished MS, Author's Collection.

Harvey, Karen. 2005. "Caleb: A Slave." *East Florida Gazette* 3–4. St. Augustine Historical Society.

Hawkins, Joseph. 1797. *A History of a Voyage to the Coast of Africa, and Travels into the Interior of that Country; containing Particular Descriptions of the Climate and Inhabitants, and interesting particulars concerning the Slave Trade.* Philadelphia: S. C. Ustick and Company.

Housewright, Wiley L. 1991. *A History of Music and Dance in Florida: 1565–1865.* Tuscaloosa: University of Alabama Press.

Hrabowski, Richard. 1809. *Directory of the District of Charleston Comprising the Place of Residence and Occupation of the White Inhabitants.* Charleston, S.C.: John Hoff.

Hurmence, Belinda. 1997. *We Lived in a Little Cabin in the Yard*. Winston Salem, N.C.: John F. Blair.

Kirk, Cooper C. 1966. "A History of the Southern Presbyterian Church in Florida: 1821–1891." PhD diss., Florida State University. Microfilm. St. Augustine Historical Society.

Klein, Martin A. 1988. "Women in Slavery in the Western Sudan." In *The End of Slavery in the Western Sudan*, edited by Suzanne Miers and Richard Roberts. Madison: University of Wisconsin Press.

Landers, Jane. 1988. "Black Society in Spanish St. Augustine, 1784–1821." PhD diss., University of Florida.

———. 1999. *Black Society in Spanish Florida*. Urbana: University of Illinois Press.

Laney, Noah. 1825. "St. Augustine Mission: Extract of a letter from Re. Noah Laney." *Methodist Magazine* 3:112–113. New York: N. Bangs and J. Emory, Methodist Printing Office.

Maguire, John E. 1906. "Historical Souvenir: Savannah Fire Department." Savannah: Rare Books Collection, Georgia Historical Society.

Mahon, John K. 1972. *The War of 1812*. Gainesville: University Press of Florida.

Mannix, Daniel P. 1976. *Black Cargoes: A History of the Atlantic Slave Trade, 1518–1865*. New York: Penguin Books.

Manucy, Albert. 1962. *The Houses of St. Augustine*. St. Augustine Historical Society.

Marotti, Frank. 2003. "Negotiating Freedom in St. Johns County, Florida, 1812–1862." PhD diss., University of Hawaii.

McGuire, William. 1991. "A Connecticut Yankee in St. Augustine, 1863." *El Escribano* 28:56–80. St. Augustine Historical Society.

McKissack, Fredrick, and Patricia McKissack. 1994. *The Royal Kingdoms of Ghana, Mali and Songhay: Life in Medieval Africa*. New York: Henry Holt.

Meier, August, and Elliot Rudwick. 1970. *From Plantation to Ghetto*, revised. New York: Farrar, Straus and Giroux.

Metraux, Alfred. 1959. *Voodoo in Haiti*. New York: Oxford University Press.

Mouser, Bruce Lee. 1971. "Trade and Politics in the Nunez & Pongo Rivers, 1790–1865." PhD diss., University of Hawaii.

———. 2002. *A Slaving Voyage to Africa and Jamaica: The Log of the Sandown, 1793–1794*. Bloomington: Indiana University Press.

New York American Missionary (NYAM). January 1866.

New York Freedmen's Advocate (NYFA). June 1864, July–August 1864, January 1865.

Palmer, Colin A. 1995. *The First Passage: Blacks in the Americas, 1562–1617*. Oxford: Oxford University Press.

Park, Mungo. 1893. *Travels in the Interior Districts of Africa: Performed in the Years 1795, 1796 & 1797*, vol. I and II. London: George Newnes.

Peck Family Papers (PFP). 1811–1887. St. Augustine Historical Society.

Pierson, William D. 1988. *Black Yankees: The Development of an Afro-American Subculture in Eighteenth Century New England*. Amherst: University of Massachusetts Press.

———. 1996. *From Africa to America: African American History from the Colonial Era to the Early Republic, 1526–1790*. New York: Twayne Publishers.

Pope-Hennessy, James. 1968. *Sins of the Fathers: A Study of the Atlantic Slave Traders, 1441–1807*. New York: Alfred A. Knopf.

Richardson, Joe M. 1864. *New York Freedman's Advocate*, June 1864, July-August 1864, January 1865.

———. 1875. "We are Truly Doing Missionary Work." Letters from American Missionary Association Teachers in Florida. *Florida Historical Quarterly* 54(2):178–195.

Richardson, Simon Peter. 1850. "Letter to the Editor." *Tallahassee Florida Sentinel*, October 15, 1850.

———. 1874. "Letter to the Editor." *Southern Christian Advocate*, March 4, 1874.

Ridley, Jasper. 2001. *The Freemasons: A History of the World's Most Powerful Secret Society*. New York: Arcade Publishing.

Rivers, Larry Eugene, and Canter Brown Jr. 2001. *Laborers in the Vineyard of the Lord: The Beginnings of the AME Church in Florida, 1865–1895*. Gainesville: University Press of Florida.

Roberts, John Storm. 1972. *Black Music of Two Worlds*. New York: Praeger.

Roque, Mariano de la. 1788. *Plano Particular de la Ciudad de San Augustin de la Florida*. Washington, D.C.: U.S. Department of the Interior, Bureau of Land Management.

Sastre, Cecile-Marie. 1990. "The British Redoubts of St. Augustine." MA thesis, Florida Atlantic University, Boca Raton, Fla.

Schafer, Daniel L. 2004. *Anna Madgigine Jai Kingsley: African Princess, Florida Slave, Plantation Owner*. Gainesville: University Press of Florida.

Sjoberg, Gideon. 1967. "The Preindustrial City." In *Peasant Society*, edited by Jack Potter, May N. Diaz, and George M. Foster. Boston: Little Brown.

Smith, Buckingham, translator. 1866. *Narratives of the Career of Hernando de Soto in the Conquest of Florida*. New York: The Bradford Club.

———. 1869. "The Story of Uncle Jack/Sitiki." Buckingham Smith Collection, Manuscript Division. New York Historical Society.

———. n.d. Untitled document on orange culture. Buckingham Smith Collection, Manuscript Division. New York Historical Society.

Smith, Jack. 1882. Obituary, Ammidon Scrapbook. St. Augustine Historical Society.

Smith, Whit. 1950. "Letter to P. P. Smith." *Tallahassee Florida Sentinel*, October 25, 1850.

St. Augustine, City of (COSA). 1824–1855. Blacks folder (BF): "Examination of Emanuel Aquai's statement relative to Charges of Insurrection Among the Negroes, May 2, 1837." St. Augustine Historical Society.

———. 1824–1855. City Council minutes (CCM), Ordinance Number One, 1853. St. Augustine Historical Society.

———. 1878–1894. Burial permits (BP). MC65: Box 1, folder 3, 1880; folder 5, 1882. St. Augustine Historical Society.

———. 1824–1855. Tax lists (TL). St. Augustine Historical Society.

———. 1825–1899. Voting records (VR): "List of Voters Polled at Municipal Election." November 15, 1872. MC17: Box 2, folder 2. St. Augustine Historical Society.

St. Augustine Examiner. 1859–1876. St. Augustine Historical Society.

St. Augustine Record. 1889–present. "Buckingham Smith Honored in Unique Dedication Rites." Microfilm. St. Augustine Historical Society.

St. Johns County (SJC) Circuit Court Records (CCR). 1821–1865. St. Augustine Historical Society.

Starling, Marion Wilson. 1988. *The Slave Narrative: Its Place in American History.* Washington, D.C.: Howard University.

Swanson, Gail. 2005. *Slave Ship Guerrero.* West Conshohocken, N.J.: Infinity Press.

Taylor, Matilda D. 1916. "Old Customs of the Early Days." *St. Augustine Record*, February 2, 1916.

Taylor, Norman. 1936. *The Garden Dictionary.* Boston: Houghton Mifflin.

Trinity Episcopal Church, St. Augustine. 1821–1845. Records of Baptisms, Confirmations, Marriages, and Burials. Microfilm. St. Augustine Historical Society.

U.S. Census. 1790–1880. St. Johns County, Florida; Charleston County, South Carolina. Washington, D.C.: U.S. Government Printing Office.

U.S. Department of the Army (DOA). 1864. South Census (SC). St. Augustine, Fla.

U.S. Statutes. 1807. II:426, #445.

U.S. War Department. 1864. William Whiting, Solicitor of the War Department, to Buckingham Smith, granting request for passage to St. Augustine from New York. St. Augustine Historical Society.

Wall, A. J. 1941. "Buckingham Smith 1810–1871." Speech delivered for Tablet Dedication at St. Augustine, Florida. St. Augustine Historical Society.

Waterbury, Jean Parker. 1999. "Defenses and Defenders: A Collection of Writings by Luis Arana." *El Escribano* 36. St. Augustine Historical Society.

Waters, Jamie Armstrong. 2004. "Passive Past Participants or Active Archaeological Agents: The Archaeology of Children in Spanish Colonial St. Augustine, Florida." PhD diss., University of Florida.

Wayne-Stites-Anderson (WSA) Family Papers. 1756–1957. Savannah: Georgia Historical Society.

Webb, Wanton S. 1885. *Webb's Historical, Industrial and Biographical Florida.* New York: W. S. Webb.

Wheeler, W. B. 1886. *The Doctrines and Discipline of the Methodist Episcopal Church, South.* Nashville, Tenn.: Southern Methodist Publishing House.

Wilks, Ivor. 1967. "Abu Bakr Al-Siddiq of Timbuktu." In *Africa Remembered: Narratives of West Africans from The Era of the Slave Trade*, edited by Philip D. Curtin. Madison: University of Wisconsin Press.

Woolson, Constance Fenimore. 1874. "The Ancient City." Part I. *Harpers New Monthly Magazine*, December 1874, L(295):1–25.

———. 1875. "The Ancient City." Part II. *Harpers New Monthly Magazine*, January 1875, L(296):165–185.

Works Projects Administration (WPA). 1940–1941. "Spanish Land Grants (SLG) in Florida," vol. 1–5.

Index

Page numbers in *italic* indicate photos or illustrations.

Patricia C. Griffin, a historic anthropologist of ethnohistory, folk cultures, and plantations in Florida, spent four decades practicing clinical mental health and teaching graduate students and is now retired from the faculty of Florida State University. She is the author of *Mullet on the Beach: The Minorcans of Florida, 1768–1788* (1991) and editor of *Fifty Years of Southeastern Archaeology: Selected Writings of John W. Griffin* (1996), both UPF books.